WILLIAMS-SONOMA

Appetizers

The Best of Williams-Sonoma Lifestyles Series

Appetizers

GENERAL EDITOR
CHUCK WILLIAMS

RECIPE PHOTOGRAPHY
RICHARD ESKITE
JOYCE OUDKERK POOL

Oxmoor House®

Contents

Introduction

All over the world, from the tapas bars of Spain and the trattorias of Italy to the dim sum restaurants of China and the sushi bars of Japan, everyday restaurants take pride in the many appetizer plates they offer, serving them either to start a meal or to be enjoyed as a meal in their own right. Indeed, what most Westerners would typically consider a first course, people in other countries often pair with a beverage for a snack or light meal at all times of the day and evening. In the following pages, you'll find a wide array of these small plates—hot and cold appetizers, salads, and soups—that can serve as a simple prelude to a main course or be grouped into menus as meals on their own.

From the countries of the Mediterranean, you'll find such classics of Spanish *tabernas* and tapas bars as tiny turnovers stuffed with sausage, thick wedges of onion-and-egg omelet, and small bowls of chilled gazpacho. Greek tavernas and Turkish *lokantas* contribute skewers of grilled poultry and flavorful dips made from yogurt or puréed chickpeas (garbanzo beans), while favorite antipasti from Italian trattorias includes thin-crusted pizzettes, piping-hot minestrone, and salads of tomatoes and mozzarella and of fresh fava (broad) beans spiked with lemon. French bistros offer an air of Gallic refinement with puréed vegetable soups and salads of simply dressed greens accompanied by a bit of cheese.

Traditional starters from eastern Europe, such as red-cabbage rolls and chilled borscht, add vibrant color and flavor to menus. And, from Mexico and South America, there is chicken tortilla soup, Brazilian shellfish soup, plump stuffed chiles, and cheese-laced quesadillas to tempt the palate.

The kitchens of Asia offer a treasure trove of appetizers and soups to the mix of international offerings, such as dim sum from China, and sushi, light broths, and crisp, refreshing salads from Japan. And from areas farther south—Thailand, Vietnam, and Indonesia—regional specialties such as grilled chicken satay, fresh spring rolls, and fragrant lemongrass-infused soups add to the Asian influence.

Such dishes are classics, prepared as they have been for generations. But other appetizers have evolved as a result of cooks mixing local foods and techniques with ingredients and methods from around the globe. In the following pages, you'll find a number of these contemporary adaptations of traditional recipes. For example, a simple butternut squash soup gets a boost from the addition of chipotle purée, crispy fingers of fried polenta take the place of French fries, and raspberry vinaigrette enlivens a salad of roasted beets.

As you read through the pages of this eclectic volume, you'll discover an inspired mix of traditional dishes and updated classics—a lively melting pot of modern-day appetizers, salads, and soups.

PLANNING A MENU

With such variety at your fingertips, deciding on the best method to serve these dishes and group them into menus can be a challenge. The recipes are organized into four easy-to-navigate chapters including hot and cold appetizers, salads, and soups. Of course, any of the recipes will work as a starter before a main dish in a conventional menu. But you can create a meal that is much more fun and satisfying if you group together a few of the recipes. These small-plates menus are ideal for nearly any occasion, from a weeknight family supper to a Saturday dinner party to a festive holiday buffet.

You can limit your menus to dishes from a particular region, such as Chinese dim sum, Italian antipasti, or Spanish tapas. But there's no reason you can't combine plates from different cuisines, as long as you keep complementary flavors and ingredients in mind. The delicate flavors of Japanese sushi, for example, would pair nicely with a crisp salad and a simple soup, but would be overwhelmed by a Mexican quesadilla or a robust Italian pasta. Shrimp and saffron pancakes are a good match with a spicy

tomato soup, but your menu would be shrimp heavy if you partnered the pancakes with a warm salad of shrimp and haricots verts.

Another golden rule of menu planning is to think seasonally. Freshness always plays an important part in the flavor—and therefore the success—of any dish, so what looks good in the market should guide you in assembling your meal. Some ingredients are available only in a specific season, which will limit when you can prepare certain dishes. For example, if a recipe calls for pea shoots or persimmons, it can only be made in spring or fall, respectively. The seasons also play a role when deciding what kind of dish to prepare. A warm salad of wild mushrooms pairs nicely with a beef barley soup for a cold-weather menu, while a chilled curried crab salad with mango sauce may be better suited to a summertime supper.

Once you've settled on your menu, you need to think about what beverages to offer. Looking to the origin of a featured recipe is usually the best approach. A Spanish red wine or sherry is the perfect companion to a selection of tapas, while a Chianti or Pinot Grigio complements most antipasti. In Asia, tea or simple broth-based soups are typically served, though beer and sake or other rice wines are also popular.

But the single most important element in planning and serving a successful menu is the enjoyment and fun you experience doing it. Be creative. Be whimsical. Think about what might make a lasting impression and don't be afraid to try it.

THE FINAL FLOURISH

A simple topping enhances the overall flavor and presentation of any dish. Croutons are among the most popular soup and salad garnishes. Garlic-infused croutons like those on page 290 are often a welcome addition, but you can also customize croutons with a specific recipe in mind. For example, croutons sautéed in basil oil yield a delightful burst of flavor in a plain tomato soup, or toasts sautéed in ginger-infused olive oil are delicious on a persimmon salad or a butternut squash soup. And if you're pressed for time, you can skip the croutons and just drizzle a thread of flavored oil onto a soup.

If you're serving spicy or other boldly flavored soups, you can temper their taste with a dollop of crème fraîche or sour cream. Or, depending on the provenance of the recipe or on the ingredients used, you can crown each bowl with a spoonful of fresh pesto, red pepper cream, or green chutney to give a new taste to an old favorite. (Look for recipes on page 290). For chilled soups, you might also try nestling the serving bowls into larger bowls filled with crushed ice as another final flourish before serving.

When you're entertaining, always take the time to garnish your appetizers—whether plated for a first course or passed on trays—with care. A fresh herb sprig is the most typical and simplest choice. Choose one or more herbs that are used in the recipe and arrange them attractively on the plate. To dress up the presentation, tie the herbs with raffia or a narrow ribbon, or add a twist of lemon or lime.

Always consider the origin of a recipe when selecting a garnish for a serving plate or platter of appetizers. For example, a knotted sheath of fresh chives or a tiny piece of lemongrass wrapped in a kaffir lime leaf and tied with a julienne strip of green (spring) onion would be appropriate for many Southeast Asian recipes. For a Mexican recipe, you might add an orange twist flanked by a tiny bouquet of fresh cilantro (coriander) to the plate. The best garnishes marry one or more ingredients used in the recipe with a healthy dose of creativity.

***

Whether you're planning a casual supper menu of two or more small plates or looking for the perfect first course before a main dish, this diverse collection of appetizers provides a broad range of options. And no matter what you choose to make, your meal will reflect the long-standing tradition of small plates found in every corner of the world.

Cold Appetizers

Baba Ghanoush

If you like, you can cook the eggplant completely in the oven instead of first blackening it on the grill. Put the eggplant in a preheated 350°F (180°C) oven and cook until soft, 30–40 minutes. Serve with warm pita wedges.

Prepare a medium-hot fire in a charcoal grill. Preheat an oven to 375°F (190°C).

Prick the eggplant with a fork in several places and place on the grill rack 4–5 inches (10–13 cm) from the fire. Grill, turning frequently, until the skin blackens and blisters and the flesh just begins to feel soft, 10–15 minutes. Transfer the eggplant to a baking sheet and bake until very soft, 15–20 minutes. Remove from the oven, let cool slightly, and peel off and discard the skin. Place the eggplant flesh in a bowl.

Using a fork, mash the eggplant to a paste. Add $1/4$ cup ($2 1/2$ oz/75 g) tahini, garlic, $1/4$ cup (2 fl oz/60 ml) lemon juice, and cumin and mix well. Season with salt, then taste and adjust with more lemon juice and/or tahini.

Transfer the mixture to a serving bowl and spread it with the back of a spoon to form a shallow well. Drizzle the olive oil over the top and sprinkle with the parsley. Place the olives around the sides. Serve at room temperature.

Serves 6

1 large eggplant (aubergine)

1/4 cup (2 1/2 oz/75 g) tahini, or to taste

3 cloves garlic, minced

1/4 cup (2 fl oz/60 ml) lemon juice, or to taste

Large pinch of ground cumin

Salt to taste

1 tablespoon extra-virgin olive oil

1 tablespoon chopped fresh flat-leaf (Italian) parsley

1/4 cup (1 1/4 oz/37 g) brine-cured black olives such as Kalamata

Bruschetta with Eggplant Caviar

Eggplant caviar is a wonderful spread to make when eggplants are plentiful in the summer. Serve the bruschetta already assembled or present each diner with an individual ramekin of caviar and a plate of toasted baguette slices to make their own.

1 large globe eggplant (aubergine) about 1 lb (500 g)

FOR THE TOASTS

2 baguettes, each cut on the diagonal into slices ½ inch (12 mm) thick

¼ cup (2 fl oz/60 ml) extra-virgin olive oil

4 cloves garlic

2 tomatoes, peeled and chopped

½ yellow onion, coarsely chopped

2 cloves garlic, coarsely chopped

1 tablespoon extra-virgin olive oil

½ cup (2½ oz/75 g) pitted and coarsely chopped Kalamata olives

¼ cup (⅓ oz/10g) coarsely chopped fresh cilantro

1–1½ tablespoons lemon juice

1 teaspoon salt

1 teaspoon ground pepper

Preheat an oven to 300°F (150°C). Place the eggplant on a baking sheet. Bake until very soft and tender when pierced with a knife and the meat pulls away from the browned skin, about 1¼ hours. Remove from the oven and let cool.

While the eggplant is cooling, prepare the toasts: Raise the temperature of the oven to 400°F (200°C). Place the baguette slices on baking sheets and drizzle them evenly with the olive oil. Bake until golden on top, about 15 minutes. Remove from the oven, turn over slices, and return to the oven. Continue to bake until golden on the second side, about 5 minutes longer. Remove from the oven. When the toasts are cool enough to handle, rub the most golden side of each one with a whole garlic clove.

When the eggplant is cool enough to handle, peel it and coarsely chop the flesh. Set aside. In a blender or food processor combine the tomatoes, onion, garlic, and olive oil. Process until smooth. Add the eggplant, olives, cilantro, lemon juice to taste, salt, and pepper. Process until smooth. You should have about 3 cups (27 oz/845 g).

To serve, spread each toast with about 1 tablespoon of the eggplant caviar and arrange on one or two platters or on individual serving plates.

Makes 48 toasts; serves 12

Crisp Vegetable Wreath with Herb-Yogurt Dip

This wreath of vegetables is a quick and healthful addition to any table. Sugar snap peas, snow peas (mangetouts), cucumbers, celery, green beans, red bell peppers (capsicums), radishes, and jicama can be substituted for the vegetables listed here.

To make the dip, in a blender, combine the onions, yogurt, cottage cheese, parsley, dill, celery salt, and the hot-pepper sauce, if using. Process on high speed until smooth and creamy, stopping to scrape down the sides of the blender as needed. Taste and adjust the seasoning with celery salt and hot-pepper sauce. Transfer to a small, shallow bowl. (The dip can be made up to 2 days ahead, covered, and refrigerated.)

Place the bowl of dip in the center of a large, round platter or tray. Surround the bowl with the cauliflower, broccoli, and tomatoes, arranging them to resemble a wreath. Garnish with the herb sprigs, if using, and serve immediately.

Serves 8

FOR THE DIP

6 green (spring) onions, white and pale green tops, coarsely chopped

1 cup (8 oz/250 g) plain yogurt

1 cup (8 oz/250 g) cottage cheese

1/4 cup (1/4 oz/7 g) loosely packed fresh flat-leaf (Italian) parsley leaves

1 tablespoon chopped fresh dill

1/2 teaspoon celery salt

2 drops hot-pepper sauce (optional)

1 small head cauliflower, trimmed and cut into florets

1 stalk broccoli, trimmed and cut into florets

About 16 cherry tomatoes, stems removed

Fresh dill and/or flat-leaf (Italian) sprigs for garnish (optional)

Turkish Tomato and Chile Relish

In summer, when tomatoes are sweet from the vine, Turkish cooks prepare this simple relish. Sometimes it is served as a salad. It is also very good with Crisp Pita Chips (page 23) or bread, accompanied by a glass of wine or raki.

3 tomatoes, about 1¼ lb (625 g) total weight, finely chopped

5 tablespoons (2½ oz/75 g) tomato paste

2 tablespoons extra-virgin olive oil

4 green Anaheim chiles, seeded and minced

½ cup (3 oz/90 g) minced yellow onion

3 tablespoons chopped fresh flat-leaf (Italian) parsley

½–1 teaspoon red pepper flakes

Salt and ground black pepper to taste

Place the tomatoes in a fine-mesh sieve set over a bowl. Let drain for 1 hour. Discard the juice or reserve for another use.

In a bowl, combine the tomatoes, tomato paste, olive oil, Anaheim chiles, onion, parsley, and the red pepper flakes to taste in a bowl. Stir to mix well. Season with salt and black pepper.

Transfer to a serving bowl and serve at room temperature.

Serves 6

Hummus

Tahini, a stiff paste made from toasted ground sesame seeds, is one of the most important ingredients in Middle Eastern cooking. Here it is used to make a garlicky chickpea purée flavored with cumin.

1¹/3 cups (9 oz/280 g) dried chickpeas (garbanzo beans)

¹/2 cup (4 fl oz/125 ml) lemon juice, or as needed

¹/2 cup (5 oz/155 g) tahini (see note)

4 tablespoons (2 fl oz/60 ml) extra-virgin olive oil

5 cloves garlic, minced

³/4 teaspoon salt, or as needed

¹/4 teaspoon ground cumin

2 teaspoons chopped fresh flat-leaf (Italian) parsley

Large pinch of paprika

6 lemon wedges or radishes

¹/4 cup (1¹/4 oz/37 g) brine-cured black olives such as Kalamata

Pick over and discard any misshapen peas or stones. Rinse the chickpeas and drain. Place in a bowl, add water to cover generously, and let soak for at least 4 hours or for up to overnight.

Drain the chickpeas and place in a saucepan with water to cover by 2 inches (5 cm). Bring to a boil over high heat, reduce the heat to low, and simmer, uncovered, until the skins crack and the chickpeas are very tender, about 1 hour. Remove from the heat and drain, reserving the liquid.

In a food processor or blender, combine the chickpeas, ¹/2 cup (4 fl oz/125 ml) lemon juice, the tahini, 3 tablespoons of the olive oil, the garlic, ³/4 teaspoon salt, and the cumin. Process until a soft, creamy paste forms. Taste and adjust with salt and lemon juice, if needed.

Transfer the purée to a serving bowl and spread with the back of a spoon to form a shallow well. Drizzle with the remaining 1 tablespoon olive oil. Sprinkle with the parsley and paprika. Garnish with the lemon wedges or radishes and the olives and serve.

Serves 6

Crisp Pita Chips

These simply delcious crisps are a traditional accompaniment to hummus, although they can also be served with a variety of Middle Eastern dips and dishes.

Preheat an oven to 375°F (190°C).

Split each pita bread into 2 rounds by carefully separating it along the outside seam. Cut each round into 6–8 wedges on a baking sheet. Drizzle with the olive oil, sprinkle with salt, and toss to coat evenly. Spread out the wedges in a single layer.

Bake, turning the wedges occasionally, until crisp, 10–12 minutes. Remove from the oven and let cool completely on the baking sheet before storing.

Makes 24–32 chips; serves 6

2 pita bread rounds, each 8 inches (20 cm) in diameter

3 tablespoons extra-virgin olive oil

Salt to taste

Yogurt Dip with Garlic, Mint, and Dill

This tangy dip is called *tzatziki* in Greece, home to some of the best yogurt in the world. You can make the dip up to 1 day in advance, but do not add the garlic. Cover and refrigerate, then add the garlic the day of serving.

Line a sieve with cheesecloth (muslin) and place over a bowl. Spoon the yogurt into the sieve and refrigerate for 4 hours to drain.

Meanwhile, using the large holes on a handheld grater-shredder, grate enough cucumber to measure 1 cup (4 oz/125 g). Spread out the grated cucumber on paper towels, salt lightly, and let drain for 15 minutes.

In a bowl, combine the yogurt, cucumber, garlic, mint, dill, olive oil, and lemon juice to taste. Stir to mix well, then season with salt.

Transfer to a bowl and serve.

Makes about 2 cups (1 lb/500 g); serves 6

2 cups (1 lb/500 g) plain yogurt

about 1/2 English (hothouse) cucumber, peeled, halved, and seeded

Salt

4 cloves garlic, mashed in a mortar or minced

1 tablespoon chopped fresh mint

1 tablespoon chopped fresh dill

1 tablespoon extra-virgin olive oil

2–3 teaspoons lemon juice

Five-Tomato Salsa

A visit to a farmers' market should provide the mix of colorful tomato varieties that this unusual salsa demands. Prepare the salsa up to 4 hours ahead and use as a dip for tortilla chips or as a topping for any of your favorite Mexican dishes.

3–4 lb (1.5–2 kg) assorted tomatoes, preferably of 5 different colors and sizes such as small and medium, red and yellow pear-shaped, cherry, and beefsteak

1 red (Spanish) or yellow onion, minced

1/2 cup (2/3 oz/20 g) chopped fresh cilantro (fresh coriander)

1 teaspoon salt

1 teaspoon ground pepper

2 tablespoons lime juice

If using cherry tomatoes, cut in half. Chop the other tomatoes into small pieces.

Place all the tomatoes in a nonaluminum bowl and add the onion, cilantro, salt, and pepper. Stir to mix, being careful not to break up the tomatoes. Add the lime juice and mix again.

Serve at once, or cover and refrigerate for up to 4 hours.

Serves 6–8

Grape Leaves Stuffed with Rice and Currants

Rinse the grape leaves in cold running water. Have ready a bowl filled with ice water. Bring a large saucepan three-fourths full of water to a boil. Add the grape leaves, a few at a time, and blanch for 1 minute. Using a slotted spoon, transfer to the ice water to cool. When all are blanched, drain and cut off the stems. Set aside.

In a large frying pan over medium heat, warm $^1/_4$ cup (2 fl oz/60 ml) of the olive oil. Add the yellow onion and cook, stirring occasionally, until soft, about 7 minutes. Add the rice, green onions, and pine nuts and stir until the green onions soften, about 3 minutes. Add the currants, parsley, mint, dill, $^3/_4$ teaspoon salt, pepper, and 1 cup (8 fl oz/250 ml) of the water. Cover and cook over low heat until the water is absorbed and the rice is cooked, about 15 minutes.

Line the bottom of a heavy 4-qt (4-l) saucepan with a few grape leaves. Sprinkle with the pinch of salt. To shape the rolled grape leaves, place a leaf, smooth side down, on a work surface. Put a heaping teaspoonful of the rice mixture near the stem end. Fold the stem end and sides over the filling and roll up toward the leaf tip. Place, seam side down, in the prepared saucepan. Continue stuffing the leaves and adding them to the pan, packing close together. When the bottom is covered, drizzle the layer with some of the remaining $^1/_4$ cup (2 fl oz/60 ml) olive oil and the lemon juice. Continue layering the stuffed grape leaves, drizzling each layer with olive oil and lemon juice, until all the filling is used. Add the remaining 1 cup (8 fl oz/250 ml) water and cover the top layer with a few leaves. Invert a small heatproof plate directly on top of the stuffed leaves. Cover the saucepan and bring to a boil over high heat. Reduce the heat to low, cover, and simmer until most of the liquid has been absorbed, about 1 $^1/_2$ hours, adding water as needed so the pan doesn't dry out. Remove from the heat and let stand in the pan for about 2 hours.

Transfer the stuffed grape leaves to a platter, garnish with lemon slices, and serve.

Makes about 60 rolled grape leaves

1 jar (1 lb/500 g) grape leaves (about 6 dozen)

$^1/_2$ cup (4 fl oz/120 ml) extra-virgin olive oil

1 large yellow onion, minced

1 cup (7 oz/220 g) long-grain white rice

12 green (spring) onions, including tender green tops, thinly sliced

$^1/_3$ cup (2 oz/60 g) pine nuts

$^1/_3$ cup (2 oz/60 g) dried currants

$^1/_4$ cup ($^1/_3$ oz/10 g) chopped fresh flat-leaf (Italian) parsley

3 tablespoons chopped fresh mint

3 tablespoons chopped fresh dill

$^3/_4$ teaspoon salt, plus a pinch of salt

$^1/_4$ teaspoon ground pepper

2 cups (16 fl oz/500 ml) water

$^1/_2$ cup (4 fl oz/125 ml) lemon juice

Lemon slices

Baby Squash in Herb and Garlic Marinade

A mixture of colorful baby summer squashes, imbued with the flavor and aroma of fresh herbs, makes a great first impression at an al fresco dinner. If round squashes are unavailable, use all zucchini.

4 baby green zucchini (courgettes)

4 baby gold zucchini (courgettes) or crookneck squashes

4 baby pattypan (custard) squashes

4 baby Ronde de Nice, scallopini, or other round summer squashes

FOR THE MARINADE

1/2 cup (4 fl oz/125 ml) olive oil

2 tablespoons red wine vinegar

3 cloves garlic, crushed

4 bay leaves

2 teaspoons *each* minced fresh thyme and minced fresh rosemary

1/2 teaspoon salt

1/2 teaspoon ground pepper

4–8 butter (Boston) or red lettuce leaves

1/2 red bell pepper (capsicum), thinly sliced

Trim the ends of the squashes but leave whole. Place on a steamer rack over boiling water, cover the steamer, and steam until tender when pierced with the tip of a knife, 2–3 minutes. Transfer to a plate.

To make the marinade, in a nonaluminum bowl, combine the olive oil, vinegar, garlic, bay leaves, thyme, rosemary, salt, and pepper; mix well. Add the squashes and turn to coat with the marinade. Cover and let stand at room temperature for 6–8 hours.

To serve, garnish 4 individual plates with a lettuce leaf or two and slices of bell pepper. Using a slotted spoon, remove the squashes from the marinade and divide them evenly among the plates. Serve at room temperature.

Serves 4

Lemon Cucumber, Tomato, and Mozzarella Rounds

Two unusual ingredients—lemon cucumbers and opal basil—lend refreshing flavor to the traditional pairing of tomato and mozzarella. Substitute 1 English (hothouse) cucumber for the lemon cucumbers and regular basil for the opal variety, if you like.

Cut the cucumbers, tomatoes, and cheese into thin slices; they should all be about the same diameter. You should have 18 slices of each.

Arrange the cucumber slices in a single layer on 1 large or 2 smaller platters. Top each cucumber slice with a tomato slice and then with a mozzarella slice. Sprinkle lightly with salt and a dusting of white pepper. Garnish each stack with a basil leaf and serve.

Serves 6

3 lemon cucumbers

4 plum (Roma) tomatoes

1/2 lb (250 g) fresh mozzarella cheese

Salt and ground white pepper to taste

18 opal basil leaves

Red Cabbage Rolls

These rolls are delicious served at room temperature accompanied with sour cream that has been seasoned with a little minced cilantro. They are best served as plated appetizers or a refreshing first course.

1 head red cabbage

Ice water as needed

1/4 cup (2 fl oz/60 ml) vegetable oil

1/2 cup (2 oz/60 g) chopped yellow onion

2 cloves garlic, minced

1 1/2 cups (12 fl oz/375 ml) vegetable broth

1/4 cup (2 fl oz/60 ml) tomato sauce

3/4 cup (5 oz/155 g) jasmine rice or other long-grain white rice

1 teaspoon red pepper flakes, or to taste

1/4 cup (1/3 oz/10 g) minced fresh flat-leaf (Italian) parsley

3 tablespoons minced fresh cilantro (fresh coriander)

1/2 teaspoon ground cumin

1/4 teaspoon ground coriander

Salt and ground pepper to taste

Remove the tough outer leaves of the cabbage and discard. Cut out the core but leave the head whole.

Bring a large pot three-fourths full of water to a boil. Immerse the cabbage in the boiling water and cook until the leaves are pliable and separate easily when gently pulled apart with tongs, 5–7 minutes. Drain and immerse immediately in ice water to stop the cooking. Drain again and blot dry with paper towels. Carefully pull apart and set aside 16 large leaves.

In a saucepan over medium heat, warm the vegetable oil. Add the onion and garlic and sauté until lightly golden, 4–5 minutes. Add the broth, tomato sauce, rice, and red pepper flakes and bring to a boil. Cover, reduce the heat to low, and cook until the rice is tender, about 30 minutes.

Remove the pan from the heat, add the parsley, cilantro, cumin, and coriander and mix well. Season with salt and pepper and set aside to cool.

Trim off the heavy rib from the base of each cabbage leaf, squaring off the end. Place a heaping tablespoon of the filling in the center of the leaf and, starting from the rib end, roll up the leaf, tucking in the sides and forming a cylinder.

Place the rolls, seam sides down, on a serving platter. Serve at room temperature.

Makes 16 rolls; serves 8

Rice Paper Rolls with Peanut Sauce

To make the sauce, in a saucepan, combine the coconut milk, peanut butter, green onion, lemongrass, garlic, lime juice, soy sauce, curry powder, coriander, and cumin. Place over medium heat and cook, stirring constantly, until well blended. Transfer to a blender or food processor and purée until smooth, thinning with water if necessary. Pour into a bowl and stir in the chile paste. Set aside.

To make the rolls, in a bowl, soak the noodles in hot water to cover for 15 minutes. Drain the noodles and cut into 2-inch (5-cm) lengths. Set aside.

In a wok or large frying pan over medium heat, warm the peanut oil. Add the garlic and cook, stirring, until lightly golden, about 2 minutes. Add the sesame oil, broccoli, and carrot and toss and stir until softened, 4–5 minutes. Add the noodles and toss and stir until the noodles are hot, 2–3 minutes. Add the bean sprouts, toss to mix and soften, then set aside to cool.

Fill a pie dish with warm water. Have ready several damp kitchen towels or sturdy paper towels. Dip 1 rice paper round at a time into the water, lay flat on a damp towel, and cover with another damp towel. Continue making layers of rice paper rounds and towels until you have used 24 rounds. Allow to soften 1–2 minutes. Transfer 1 round to a work surface and place a heaping tablespoon of filling in the middle. Top with a few mint and cilantro leaves. Turn up 2 sides and roll into a cylinder. Continue with the remaining rounds.

Line a platter with lettuce leaves and arrange the rolls on top. Serve with the peanut sauce.

Makes 24 rolls; serves 8

FOR THE PEANUT SAUCE

1/2 cup (4 fl oz/125 ml) *each* coconut milk and peanut butter

1 green (spring) onion, minced

1 piece lemongrass stalk, 3 inches (7.5 cm) long, minced

2 cloves garlic, minced

juice of 1/2 lime

1 tablespoon soy sauce

1 teaspoon *each* curry powder and ground coriander

1/2 teaspoon ground cumin

1 teaspoon chile paste

FOR THE ROLLS

1/2 lb (250 g) dried rice stick noodles

3 tablespoons peanut oil

1 clove garlic, minced

1/2 teaspoon Asian sesame oil

1/2 lb (250 g) Chinese broccoli, trimmed and coarsely chopped

1 carrot, peeled and coarsely grated

1/2 cup (1 oz/30 g) bean sprouts

24 rice paper rounds, 6 inches (15 cm) in diameter

Fresh mint and fresh cilantro (fresh coriander) leaves

Butter (Boston) lettuce leaves

Smoked Salmon with Mustard-Dill Potatoes

Nearly any type of smoked salmon will work well in this delicous and satisfying appetizer. For a special occasion, use good-quality Scottish smoked salmon. Serve with pumpernickel toast points, if desired.

1¼ lb (625 g) baby red new potatoes

⅓ cup (3 oz/90 g) fromage blanc

2½ tablespoons chopped fresh dill, plus sprigs for garnish (optional)

1 teaspoon mustard seeds

Ground pepper to taste

¼ cup (2 oz/60 g) Dijon mustard

¼ cup (2 fl oz/60 ml) fat-free sour cream

1½ tablespoons sugar

4 teaspoons white wine vinegar

½ lb (250 g) thinly sliced smoked salmon

Fresh dill sprigs (optional)

Place the potatoes in a saucepan with boiling water to cover. Reduce the heat to medium and simmer, uncovered, until just tender, about 20 minutes. Drain and transfer to a work surface.

Meanwhile, in a small bowl, combine the fromage blanc, ½ tablespoon of the chopped dill, and the mustard seeds and stir until smooth. Season with pepper and set aside.

In a bowl, stir together the mustard, sour cream, the remaining 2 tablespoons dill, sugar, and vinegar. Cut the potatoes into slices ¼ inch (6 mm) thick, add to the mustard mixture, and toss gently to coat. Season with pepper.

Transfer the potatoes to individual plates, dividing them evenly. Top with the salmon; drizzle the fromage blanc mixture on top of the salmon. Garnish with dill sprigs, if desired.

Serves 4

Mushrooms Cooked with Garlic

This traditional Spanish *tapas* dish is often made with the wild mushrooms prevalent there in the Fall and again in the Spring. Here, small button mushrooms are substituted with excellent results.

1 cup (8 fl oz/250ml) dry white wine

1 cup (8 fl oz/250 ml) white wine vinegar

¼ cup (2 fl oz/60 ml) extra-virgin olive oil

12 cloves garlic, thinly sliced

4 bay leaves

¼ teaspoon red pepper flakes

large pinch of saffron threads

2 teaspoons salt

1 teaspoon ground black pepper

2½ (1.25 kg) fresh small button mushrooms, brushed clean

1 tablespoon chopped fresh flat-leaf (Italian) parsley

In a saucepan, combine the wine, vinegar, olive oil, garlic, bay leaves, red pepper flakes, saffron, salt, and black pepper. Place over high heat and bring to a boil. Reduce the heat to medium-low, cover, and simmer until the liquid thickens slightly and forms a flavorful stock, about 30 minutes. Remove from the heat and pour through a fine-mesh sieve placed over a bowl, pressing against the contents of the sieve with the back of a wooden spoon to extract as much liquid as possible. Return the liquid to the saucepan. Discard the solids.

Add the mushrooms to the liquid in the saucepan along with enough water almost to cover them. Bring to a boil over high heat, reduce the heat to medium-low, and simmer, uncovered, stirring occasionally, until the mushrooms are tender, about 3 minutes. Using a slotted spoon, transfer the mushrooms to a bowl. Place the cooking liquid over high heat and boil, uncovered, until reduced to $^1/_2$ cup (4 fl oz/125 ml), 5–10 minutes. Pout the hot liquid over the mushrooms, mix well, and let cool completely. Cover and refrigerate overnight.

About 30 minutes before serving, remove the mushrooms from the refrigerator and bring to room temperature. Garnish with the parsley.

Serves 6

Cherry Tomatoes with Goat Cheese

For a refreshing summertime appetizer, fill bite-sized cherry tomatoes, round or pear shaped, with a savory mixture of goat cheese flavored with basil. Minced tarragon or chervil can be used in place of the basil.

Cut the top off each cherry tomato. Using a small spoon, scoop out the pulp to make a hollow yet sturdy shell. Drain off any juice that accumulates in the shells.

In a bowl, combine the cheese, basil, salt, and pepper. Mix with a fork until well blended.

Using the small spoon, fill each tomato with about 1 teaspoon of the cheese mixture. Arrange the filled tomatoes on a platter to serve.

Makes 24 pieces; serves 4

24 cherry tomatoes, a mixture of red and yellow

1/4 lb (125 g) fresh goat cheese

1/4 cup (1/3 oz/10 g) minced fresh basil

1/2 teaspoon salt

1/2 teaspoon ground pepper

Spring Rolls with Salmon and Mango

Place the noodles in a bowl and add water to cover. Let stand until soft and pliable, about 15 minutes. Bring a large pot two-thirds full of water to a boil. Drain the noodles, add to the boiling water, remove from the heat, and let stand for 2 minutes. Drain and rinse with cold water. Drain thoroughly and set aside.

Pour water to a depth of 3 inches (7.5 cm) in a wide, deep frying pan and bring to just below a boil over high heat. Slip the salmon into the water and poach until the flesh easily flakes with a fork, 5–10 minutes. Transfer the salmon to a plate and refrigerate for 1 hour. Cut into 16 thin slices about 4 inches (10 cm) long.

In a small bowl, combine the carrot and sugar. Let stand until the carrot is softened, about 10 minutes.

Fill a pie dish with warm water. Have ready several damp kitchen towels or sturdy paper towels. Dip 1 rice paper round at a time into the water, lay flat on a damp towel, and cover with another damp towel. Continue making layers of rice paper rounds and towels until you have used 16 rounds. Allow to soften 1–2 minutes. Transfer 1 round to a work surface and place 1 lettuce leaf across the lower third of the round, leaving a 1-inch (2.5-cm) border on both sides. Spread a small amount (about one-sixteenth) of the noodles over the lettuce. Arrange one-sixteenth of the carrots, a few mango slices, a salmon slice, a few avocado slices, and a few shreds of mint over the noodles. Fold up the bottom edge of the rice paper round and roll once over the ingredients, tucking them into a tight roll 5 inches (13 cm) long. Fold in both sides to enclose the filling. Place 2 sprigs of cilantro over the roll and finish rolling. Set, seam side down, on a baking sheet, cover with a damp kitchen towel, and set in a cool spot while making the remaining rolls. Serve at room temperature with the dipping sauce.

Makes 16 rolls; serves 8

4 oz (125 g) dried thin rice vermicelli noodles

1 lb (500 g) salmon fillets

1 large carrot, peeled and very finely julienned

1 teaspoon sugar

16 dried rice paper rounds, each 8 1/2 inches (21.5 cm) in diameter

16 large red-leaf lettuce leaves, ribs removed

1 mango, peeled and cut into slices 3–4 inches (7.5–10 cm) long and 1/4 inch (6 mm) thick

1 avocado, pitted, peeled, and cut into slices 3–4 inches (7.5–10 cm) long and 1/4 inch (6 mm) thick

16 fresh mint leaves, shredded

32 sprigs of fresh cilantro (fresh coriander)

Garlic-Lime Dipping Sauce (page 290)

Tuna Tartare

Serve this spicy seafood specialty with lightly toasted French bread or with quickly fried *pappadams* from India. A light, fruity rosé or a sparkling wine also makes a wonderful accompaniment.

1 lb (500 g) sashimi-quality tuna fillet, preferably bigeye or yellowfin, cut into 1/4-inch (6-mm) dice

1/4 cup (1 1/2 oz/45 g) finely minced red (Spanish) onion

1 1/2 tablespoons minced green or red jalapeño chile, seeded if desired

2 tablespoons finely minced green (spring) onion, including tender green tops

2 teaspoons grated lemon zest

1/4 cup (2 fl oz/60 ml) olive oil

3 tablespoons Asian sesame oil

Kosher or sea salt and coarsely ground pepper to taste

1 lemon, quartered

In a bowl, carefully and gently combine the tuna, red onion, chile, green onion, lemon zest, olive oil, and sesame oil. Season generously with salt and pepper.

Mound the tuna mixture on individual plates and serve immediately with lemon wedges alongside.

Serves 4

Buckwheat Noodles with Dipping Sauce

This Japanese noodle dish, *zaru soba*, is traditionally presented in slatted bamboo boxes or baskets to ensure perfectly drained noodles. Using flat soup bowls makes an equally elegant presentation. Nori seaweed is available already toasted and shredded.

To make the dipping sauce, using a damp kitchen towel, wipe, but do not wash, the kombu. In a saucepan over medium heat, combine the kombu and the water. Slowly bring almost to a boil, then remove the kombu. Return the water to a boil over medium-high heat, add the soy sauce, mirin, and sugar, and bring just to a boil. Add the bonito flakes; do not stir. Immediately remove from the heat and let stand until the flakes sink to the bottom of the pan, about 10 minutes. Pour through a fine-mesh sieve into a bowl. Cover and refrigerate for 1 hour or for up to 2 days.

Bring a large pot three-fourths full of water to a boil. Add the noodles, stirring to separate the strands, and bring to a boil. Reduce the heat to medium-high and cook, stirring occasionally, until tender but firm to the bite, 3–5 minutes or according to the package directions. Drain, rinse thoroughly with cold running water, and divide among 6 bowls. Cover and set aside.

In a small bowl, combine the wasabi powder and water. Stir to form a smooth paste and set aside for 10 minutes. Rinse the green onions under cold running water and gently squeeze to remove excess moisture and any bitter flavor.

To serve, sprinkle the shredded nori over the noodles, dividing evenly. Pour the dipping sauce into 6 small bowls. Arrange equal amounts of wasabi, green onions, and daikon in 6 small condiment dishes.

Serves 6

FOR THE DIPPING SAUCE

1 piece kombu seaweed, about 3 inches (7.5 cm) long

3 cups (24 fl oz/750 ml) water

1/2 cup (4 fl oz/125 ml) soy sauce

1/4 cup (2 fl oz/60 ml) mirin

1 teaspoon sugar

3 1/2 cups (1 3/4 oz/50 g) loosely packed bonito flakes

3/4 lb (375 g) dried buckwheat (soba) noodles

2 tablespoons wasabi powder

4 1/2 teaspoons water

6 green (spring) onions, including tender green tops, minced

1/4 cup (1/4 oz/7 g) finely shredded toasted nori seaweed

6 tablespoons grated daikon

California Rolls

3 1/2 cups (1 1/2 lb/750 g) short-grain rice, well rinsed

3 3/4 cups (30 fl oz/940 ml) cold water

1/3 cup (3 fl oz/80 ml) plus 1 1/2 tablespoons water

2 teaspoons plus 1/2 cup (4 fl oz/125 ml) unseasoned rice vinegar

2 tablespoons wasabi powder

1/3 cup (3 oz/90 g) sugar

1 teaspoon salt

6 sheets toasted nori seaweed, about 7 by 8 inches (18 by 20 cm)

1/4 cup (1 oz/30 g) sesame seeds, toasted in a dry frying pan for 3–5 minutes

3/4 English (hothouse) cucumber, peeled and cut into thin strips 6 inches (15 cm) long

1 1/2 avocadoes, pitted, peeled, and cut into slices 1/4 inch (6 mm) thick

6 oz (185 g) cooked fresh crabmeat, flaked into pieces

1/2 cup (4 fl oz/125 ml) Japanese soy sauce for dipping

3/4 cup (5 oz/155 g) pickled ginger slices

In a 3-qt (3-l) saucepan, bring the rice and water to a boil over high heat. Cook, uncovered, stirring occasionally, for 3 minutes. Cover, reduce the heat to low, and cook, without stirring, until tender, about 20 minutes. Set aside for 10 minutes.

In a small bowl, combine the 1/3 cup (3 fl oz/80 ml) water and 2 teaspoons vinegar. In another small bowl, combine the wasabi powder and 1 1/2 tablespoons water, stir to form a smooth paste, and let stand for 10 minutes. Divide in half and set half aside. In a small saucepan over low heat, combine the 1/2 cup (4 oz/125 ml) vinegar, the sugar, and the salt and cook, stirring occasionally, until the sugar and salt are dissolved, about 3 minutes. Set aside to cool.

Transfer the hot rice to a large bowl. Drizzle with two-thirds of the vinegar-sugar mixture and gently fold into the rice. Add only as much as the rice will absorb without becoming mushy. Cover with a damp kitchen towel.

Place a bamboo sushi mat on a work surface with the bamboo strips running horizontally. Place 1 nori sheet horizontally, shiny side down, on the mat, aligned with the edge nearest you. Dip your hands into the vinegar-water mixture and spread about 2 cups (10 oz/315 g) of the rice in an even layer over the nori sheet, leaving the top one-fourth uncovered. Smear a thin strip of wasabi horizontally across the middle. Sprinkle sesame seeds over the wasabi, followed by a few cucumber strips, an even row of avocado slices, and one-sixth of the crabmeat. Lift the nearest edge of the bamboo mat, nori, and rice over the filling to seal it inside. Continue to roll the mat away from you, pressing to form a snug cylinder about 2 inches (5 cm) thick. Dipping a sharp knife in water before each cut, cut the roll in half. Cut each half into 4 equal pieces. Repeat with the remaining 5 nori sheets.

Serve the sushi with the reserved wasabi, the soy sauce, and the pickled ginger. Provide small dishes for mixing wasabi with soy sauce for use as a dipping sauce.

Makes 24 pieces; serves 6

Smoked Herring and Cream Cheese Pâté with Dill

Smoked herring, sometimes called kippers, are fresh herring that have been split, salted, dried, and then cold smoked. The smoky taste of the fish and the creaminess of the cheese make this a sophisticated appetizer for entertaining.

In a food processor, combine the smoked herring, cream cheese, shallots, lemon juice, snipped dill, and lemon zest. Process until smooth. Scrape into a bowl, cover, and chill for about 1 hour.

Meanwhile, trim the bases from the endives, and separate the leaves. You will need 24 leaves. Place in a bowl, add cold water just to cover, and drop in a few ice cubes. Refrigerate until ready to use.

When the pâté is chilled, drain the leaves, pat them dry, and spoon 1 generous tablespoon of the pâté onto each leaf. Alternatively, spoon the chilled pâté into a pastry (piping) bag fitted with a large rosette tip, and pipe a rosette in the center of the leaf or pipe a strip along the length of the leaf. If desired, garnish each leaf with a dill sprig and a small spoonful of salmon caviar.

Arrange the filled leaves on a platter and serve, or cover and refrigerate for up to 3 hours before serving. Serve chilled.

Makes 24 pieces; serves 8–12

½ lb (250 g) smoked herring, patted dry, larger bones and skin removed, and fish broken into pieces

1 lb (500 g) cream cheese, at room temperature

¼ cup (1 oz/30 g) chopped shallots

2 tablespoons lemon juice

2 tablespoons snipped fresh dill, plus sprigs for garnish (optional)

1 teaspoon grated lemon zest

2 or 3 heads Belgian endive (chicory/witloof)

Salmon caviar (optional)

Hot Appetizers

Fava Bean and Jalapeño Wontons

The meaty flavor of fresh fava beans marries well with the spicy heat of jalapeño chiles. These crispy wontons can be served plain or with a spicy chutney, such as mango or peach, for dipping.

Place the fava beans in a saucepan and add water to cover and the salt. Bring to a boil and cook until very tender, about 5 minutes. (If the beans are large and mature, they will require longer cooking.) Drain and rinse with cold running water to halt the cooking. Using the tip of a knife or a fingernail, slit the thin skin surrounding each bean and slip it off. Transfer the peeled beans to a blender or food processor. Add the cream, mint, and pepper and purée until smooth.

Lay a wonton wrapper on a flat surface and place 1 tablespoon of the purée in the center. Top with a jalapeño slice. Dip a finger in water and run a bead of moisture around the edge of the wrapper. Fold to form a triangle and press the edges to seal. Repeat until all the purée is used, placing the filled wontons on a piece of waxed paper or aluminum foil. (Leftover wonton wrappers can be wrapped well and refrigerated for up to 2 weeks.)

Pour oil into a deep-fat fryer, wok, or deep saucepan to a depth of 4 inches (10 cm). Heat to 350°F (180°C) on a deep-fat frying thermometer. When the oil is hot, add a few wontons and fry until golden brown, 2–3 minutes. Using tongs or a slotted spoon, transfer to paper towels to drain; keep warm. Fry the remaining wontons in the same manner.

Transfer the wontons to a platter and serve hot or at room temperature.

Makes 24 wontons; serves 6–8

4 lb (2 kg) young, tender fava (broad) beans, shelled

1 teaspoon salt

1 tablespoon heavy (double) cream

1 tablespoon chopped fresh mint

1 teaspoon ground pepper

1 package (8 oz/250 g) wonton wrappers

4 jalapeño chiles, seeded and thinly sliced

Canola, sunflower, or other light oil for deep-frying

Caramelized Onion Tortilla

This Spanish tortilla is a cousin to the Italian frittata. In Spain, it is called a *tortilla de cebolla*, as opposed to the more common *tortilla Espanola* made with potatoes. Like all the tortillas of Spain, however, it is cut into wedges for serving.

4 tablespoons (2 fl oz/60 ml) olive oil

3 lb (1.5 kg) yellow onions, finely chopped

6 eggs

Salt and ground pepper to taste

Fresh sage leaves (optional)

In a frying pan over medium heat, warm 2 tablespoons of the olive oil. Add the onions and stir to combine. Cover and cook until softened, about 15 minutes, stirring once halfway through. Uncover, stir, and reduce the heat to low. Re-cover and continue to cook, stirring occasionally, until very soft and golden, about 1 hour. Remove from the heat and let cool for 10 minutes.

In a bowl, whisk together the eggs, salt, and pepper until blended. Stir in the onions.

In a 10-inch (25-cm) nonstick frying pan over medium heat, warm the remaining 2 tablespoons oil just until it begins to smoke. Pour the egg-onion mixture in the the pan and cook, occasionally loosening the edges with a spatula to allow the uncooked portion to run underneath and form a high, rounded edge. When the eggs are almost set, after 10–12 minutes, invert a plate over the top of the frying pan. Holding them together firmly, flip the plate and pan so the tortilla falls onto the plate. Slide the tortilla back into the frying pan, browned side up. Cook until browned on the bottom, 4–5 minutes. It should be slightly soft in the center.

Slide the tortilla out onto a serving plate. Let stand for 10 minutes, then cut into wedges. Serve hot, warm, or at room temperature. Garnish with sage leaves, if desired.

Serves 6

Green Olive and Manchego Puffs

Spanish appetizers, or *tapas*, often feature one of the many varieties of Spanish sausage. The most popular type is undoubtedly chorizo, made from pork and spiced with cumin, garlic, and paprika. The last is what gives the sausage its deep red color.

Sift the flour into a bowl. Add the red pepper flakes and stir to mix well. Make a well in the center. Separate the eggs, placing the yolks in a small bowl and the whites in a medium bowl. Beat the yolks with a fork just until blended and pour into the well in the flour. Add the beer, olive oil, salt, and black pepper. Using a spoon, mix well, but do not overmix or the batter will get stringy. Cover and let stand at room temperature for 1 hour.

In a deep, heavy saucepan, pour in oil to a depth of 2 inches (5 cm) and heat to 375°F (190°C) on a deep-frying thermometer.

While the oil is heating, place the chorizo in a frying pan over medium heat and break it up with a wooden spoon. Cooking, stirring occasionally, until heated through, 3–4 minutes. At the same time, using an electric mixer, beat the egg whites until stiff peaks form.

Fold in the egg whites, chorizo, cheese, olives, and chopped parsley into the batter. Working in batches, drop the batter by heaping tablespoonfuls into the hot oil; do not crowd the pan. Fry, turning occasionally, until golden, 2–3 minutes. Using a slotted spoon, transfer to paper towels and drain. Keep warm. Arrange the puffs on a warmed platter and serve immediately.

Makes about 30 puffs; serves 8–10

1 cup (5 oz/155 g) all-purpose (plain) flour

1/4 teaspoon red pepper flakes

3 eggs

3/4 cup (6 fl oz/180 ml) beer, at room temperature

2 tablespoons olive oil

1/2 teaspoon salt

Pinch of ground black pepper

Peanut or corn oil for deep-frying

10 oz (315 g) chorizo sausages, casings removed

1/2 cup (2 oz/60g) grated manchego or Parmesan cheese

1/3 cup (2 oz/60 g) Spanish brine-cured green olives, pitted and chopped

3 tablespoons chopped fresh flat-leaf (Italian) parsley

Mozzarella in Carrozza

Cut into strips, this Italian cheese sandwich makes a terrific antipasto. If you like, slip some chopped olives, a pinch of red pepper flakes, or chopped sun-dried tomatoes between the bread slices along with the cheese.

5 eggs

3 tablespoons milk

1 teaspoon salt

$1/2$ loaf coarse country bread, about $1/2$ lb (250 g), cut into slices $1/2$ inch (12 mm) thick

1 lb (500 g) fresh mozzarella cheese, cut into slices $1/4$ inch (6 mm) thick

Olive oil for frying

In a large, shallow bowl, beat together the eggs, milk, and salt until blended.

Using 2 slices of bread and 1 slice of cheese for each, make as many cheese sandwiches as you can. One at a time, dip the sandwiches into the egg mixture, coating evenly.

In a deep, heavy frying pan over medium-high heat, pour in olive oil to a depth of $1/4$ inch (6 mm) and warm over medium-high heat just until it begins to ripple. In batches, place the sandwiches in the hot oil in a single layer and cook, pressing down on the tops with a spatula and turning once, until golden, about 1 minute on each side. Using a slotted spatula or tongs, transfer to paper towels to drain. Keep warm until all the sandwiches are cooked.

Cut the sandwiches into strips 1 inch (2.5 cm) wide and arrange on a platter. Serve immediately.

Makes about 24 pieces; serves 6–8

Bite-Sized Rice Croquettes

These tiny croquettes, crispy on the outside and creamy inside, are a specialty of northern Italy. They can be prepared up to 3 days in advance, covered, and refrigerated. Deep-fry just before serving.

In a saucepan over medium heat, warm the olive oil. Add the onion and cook, stirring occasionally, until soft, about 7 minutes. Add the rice and continue to cook, stirring constantly, until coated with oil and hot, about 2 minutes.

Meanwhile, in a saucepan over medium heat, combine the broth and milk and bring just to a simmer. Immediately add the milk-broth mixture to the rice with $^{1}/_{3}$ cup ($2^{1}/_{2}$ oz/75 g) of the olive paste and the salt and pepper. Bring to a simmer, reduce the heat to low, cover, and cook until all the liquid has been absorbed and the rice is tender, about 20 minutes. Stir in the remaining $^{1}/_{3}$ cup ($2^{1}/_{2}$ oz/75 g) olive paste and the cheese. Remove from the heat and let cool completely, about 1 hour.

Using a scant tablespoon of the rice mixture for each croquette, form the mixture into balls the size of large olives, about 1 inch (2.5 cm) in diameter. Place the flour in a shallow bowl. In another bowl, whisk together the eggs and water until blended. Place the bread crumbs in a third bowl. Roll the rice balls in the flour, then in the egg, and finally in the bread crumbs, coating evenly each time. As the balls are coated, place on a baking sheet.

In a deep frying pan or a saucepan, pour in equal parts vegetable oil and olive oil to a depth of 1 inch (2.5 cm) and heat to 375°F (190°C) on a deep-frying thermometer. Add the balls, in batches, and fry, turning as needed, until golden on all sides, 1–1$^{1}/_{2}$ minutes. Using a slotted spoon, transfer to a wire rack placed over a paper towel–lined tray to drain. Keep warm until all of the balls are cooked. Arrange on a platter and serve immediately.

Makes 60 croquettes; serves 12

2 tablespoons extra-virgin olive oil

$^{1}/_{2}$ small yellow onion, minced

1 cup (7 oz/220 g) Arborio rice

$1^{1}/_{4}$ cups (10 fl oz/310 ml) chicken broth

$1^{1}/_{4}$ cups (10 fl oz/310 ml) milk

$^{2}/_{3}$ cup (5 oz/150 g) black olive paste

Salt and ground pepper to taste

$^{1}/_{4}$ cup (1 oz/30 g) grated Parmesan cheese

1 cup (5 oz/155 g) all-purpose (plain) flour

4 eggs

$^{1}/_{2}$ cup (4 fl oz/125 ml) water

4 cups (1 lb/500 g) fine dried bread crumbs

Vegetable oil and olive oil for deep-frying

Artichoke Slivers with Thyme and Marjoram

Herb-strewn artichokes, seasoned with the flavors of the Mediterranean,
make a simple yet elegant first course. Pair them with a creamy, garlicky
mayonnaise as part of an antipasto plate.

4 lemons

12 medium artichokes

1/4 cup (2 fl oz/60 ml) extra-virgin olive oil

2 tablespoons minced fresh thyme

2 tablespoons minced fresh marjoram

1 teaspoon salt

1 teaspoon ground pepper

Preheat an oven to 350°F (180°C).

Fill a large bowl three-fourths full with water. Halve 2 of the lemons and squeeze their juice into the water. Working with 1 artichoke at a time, cut off the stem flush with the base. Break off the tough outer leaves to reach the tender inner leaves. Trim away the tough, dark green layer around the base. Cut off the top one-third of each artichoke. Cut the artichokes in half lengthwise and, using the edge of a small spoon, scoop out and discard the furry inner choke from each half. Place the trimmed halves in the lemon water. When all the artichokes are trimmed, remove the halves one by one and cut lengthwise into slivers 1/4 inch (6 mm) thick. Return to the water until all the artichokes are prepared.

Drain the artichokes, wrap in a kitchen towel, and pat dry. In a bowl, combine the olive oil, thyme, marjoram, salt, and pepper. Add the artichokes and turn in the oil mixture to coat well.

Spread the artichoke mixture on a nonstick baking sheet. Roast, turning occasionally, until the artichokes are lightly browned and thoroughly tender, 30–40 minutes.

To serve, transfer the artichokes to a platter. Cut the remaining 2 lemons into wedges and use to garnish the platter. Serve hot or at room temperature.

Serves 4–6

Spicy Potato Fritters

These delicous fritters, crisp on the outside and soft in the middle, are best served alongside Indian Green Chutney (page 290). Garam masala is an Indian spice blend. To make your own, consult the glossary (page 293).

Prepare the chutney, if you like. Set aside.

Preheat an oven to 250°F (120°C). In a bowl, combine the chickpea flour, broth, 1 tablespoon peanut oil, garam masala, turmeric, and baking powder. Stir until well mixed. Stir in the green onions, chile, and cilantro. The batter should be thick. Season with salt and pepper.

Pour peanut oil into a large frying pan to a depth of 1 inch (2.5 cm) and heat over medium heat to 350°F (180°C) on a deep-fat frying thermometer. Meanwhile, peel and thinly slice the yam or sweet potato and the baking potato. Working in batches, dip the slices into the batter to coat and then slip them into the hot oil. Fry, turning once, until golden brown on both sides, 3–5 minutes on each side. Using a slotted spoon or tongs, transfer to paper towels to drain. Keep warm until all are cooked.

Transfer to a warmed serving platter and serve with the chutney, if desired.

Serves 8

Indian Green Chutney (page 290), optional

1 cup (5½ oz/170 g) chickpea (garbanzo bean) flour

1 cup (8 fl oz/250 ml) vegetable broth or water

1 tablespoon peanut oil, plus oil for frying

1 tablespoon garam masala

½ teaspoon ground turmeric

½ teaspoon baking powder

2 green (spring) onions, minced

1 serrano chile, minced

2 tablespoons minced fresh cilantro (fresh coriander)

Salt and ground pepper to taste

1 yam or sweet potato

1 baking potato

Pizzetta with Tomatoes and Mozzarella

If you are short of time, substitute 1 pound (500 g) store-bought pizza dough for the homemade. You can make the dough a day in advance and let it rise overnight in the refrigerator. Bring to room temperature before shaping.

FOR THE DOUGH

1½ teaspoons active dry yeast

3 tablespoons warm water (115°F/46°C)

3 tablespoons plus 1¼ cups (6½ oz/ 200 g) all-purpose (plain) or bread (hard-wheat) flour

¼ teaspoon salt

½ cup (4 fl oz/125 ml) cold water

1 tablespoon milk

1 tablespoon extra-virgin olive oil

2 cups (12 oz/375 g) peeled, seeded, and chopped tomatoes (fresh or canned)

Salt and ground pepper to taste

¼ lb (125 g) fresh mozzarella cheese, coarsely shredded

To make the dough, in a bowl, using a wooden spoon, stir together the yeast, warm water, and the 3 tablespoons flour. Let stand until foamy, about 20 minutes. Add the 1¼ cups (6½ oz/200 g) flour, salt, cold water, milk, and olive oil and stir until the dough pulls away from the sides of the bowl. Turn out onto a floured work surface and knead until soft, supple, and smooth yet still moist, 7–10 minutes. Place the dough in an oiled bowl, turning to coat with oil. Cover the bowl with plastic wrap, transfer to a warm place and let the dough rise until doubled in bulk, 1–2 hours.

Meanwhile, in a nonstick frying pan over medium-high heat, bring the tomatoes to a boil. Reduce the heat to low and simmer until the consistency of tomato paste, 30–40 minutes. Remove from the heat, season with salt and pepper, and let cool.

About 45 minutes before serving, place a pizza stone or baking tiles on the bottom rack of an oven and preheat to 500°F (260°C).

On a floured surface, punch down the dough and divide in half. Shape each half into a smooth ball. Roll out 1 ball into a round about 7 inches (18 cm) in diameter. Transfer the round to a well-floured pizza peel or a rimless baking sheet. Spread half of the tomatoes over the surface to within ½ inch (12 mm) of the edge. Sprinkle evenly with half of the cheese. Slide the dough round onto the heated stone or tiles and bake until golden brown and crisp on the bottom, 8–10 minutes. Carefully slip the peel or baking sheet under the pizzetta and transfer to a cutting board. Repeat with the remaining dough and topping ingredients. While the second pizzetta is baking, cut the first pizzetta into 6 wedges and serve.

Makes two 7-inch (18-cm) rounds; serves 6

Stuffed Anaheim Chiles with Creamy Guacamole

The guacamole sauce in this lively summertime first is an elegant variation on the famed dip found in Mexican restaurants on both sides of the border. If you prefer a slightly spicier dish, use poblanos and sprinkle each serving with a little chili powder.

To make the guacamole sauce, in a blender or food processor, combine the avocados, sour cream, broth, and lemon zest. Process until smooth. Transfer to a bowl and season with salt, pepper, and red pepper flakes. Set aside.

Preheat a broiler (griller). Place the chiles on a baking sheet. Broil (grill), turning as needed, until the skins blacken and blister. Remove from the broiler, drape loosely with aluminum foil, and let cool for 10 minutes, then peel away the skins. Make a lengthwise slit in each chile and carefully remove the seeds. Leave the stems intact and try to maintain the shape of the chiles. Set the chiles aside.

Preheat an oven to 375°F (190°C). Lightly oil a baking sheet.

To make the filling, in a sauté pan over medium heat, warm the olive oil. Add the onion and garlic and sauté until softened, about 3 minutes. Raise the heat to medium-high, pour in the broth, and deglaze the pan, stirring with a wooden spoon to dislodge any browned bits from the pan bottom. Add the rice, reduce the heat to low, and simmer until the liquid is absorbed, 10–15 minutes. Stir in the tomatoes and cilantro and heat through. Add the cheese and season with salt and pepper. Remove from the heat.

Spoon the filling into the chiles, packing them well and keeping their shape. Place on the prepared baking sheet, slit sides up, cover with aluminum foil, and bake until the cheese is melted, about 20 minutes.

To serve, transfer each chile to a warmed plate. Pass the guacamole at the table.

Serves 8

FOR THE CREAMY GUACAMOLE

2 ripe avocados, pitted and peeled

1/2 cup (4 fl oz/125 ml) sour cream

1/2 cup (4 fl oz/125 ml) vegetable broth

1 teaspoon grated lemon zest

Salt, ground pepper, and red pepper flakes to taste

FOR THE CHILES

8 Anaheim chiles

3 tablespoons olive oil

1 red (Spanish) onion, minced

3 cloves garlic, minced

1 1/4 cups (10 fl oz/310 ml) vegetable broth

1/2 cup (3 1/2 oz/105 g) medium-grain white rice

2 plum (Roma) tomatoes, peeled, seeded, and diced

2 tablespoons minced fresh cilantro (fresh coriander)

1/2 cup (2 oz/60 g) shredded cheddar cheese

Salt and ground pepper to taste

Crisp Potatoes with Allioli

Catalan allioli is the Iberian equivalent of Provençal *aiolo*, or garlic mayonnaise. Drizzled over hot, crisp potatoes, it melts into them, creating a rich, creamy sauce for this traditional Spanish tapas dish.

3 lb (1.5 kg) small red potatoes, unpeeled

1 tablespoon olive oil

Salt and ground pepper to taste

FOR THE ALLIOLI

½ cup (4 fl oz/125 ml) olive oil

½ cup (4 fl oz/125 ml) vegetable, safflower, or corn oil

1 egg yolk

4 cloves garlic minced

2 tablespoons white wine vinegar

Coarse salt and ground pepper to taste

1–2 tablespoons warm water

Position a rack in the upper third of an oven and preheat to 375°F (190°C).

Halve the potatoes crosswise and place in a baking dish large enough to hold them in a single layer. Drizzle with the olive oil and sprinkle with salt and pepper. Toss to coat evenly, then arrange in a single layer. Bake until golden, tender, and crispy, about 45–55 minutes.

Meanwhile, make the allioli: In a small bowl, combine the two oils. In another bowl, whisk together the egg yolk and 1 tablespoon of the combined oils until an emulsion forms. Drop by drop, add the remaining oil mixture to the egg emulsion, whisking constantly. Do not add the oil too quickly, and be sure that the emulsion is set before adding more oil. Season with the garlic, vinegar, coarse salt, and pepper. Whisking constantly, add as much of the warm water as need to create a smooth, thick consistency.

To serve, place the potatoes on a serving platter and pour half of the allioli over the top. (Cover and refrigerate the remaining allioli and reserve for another use.) Serve immediately.

Serves 6

Quesadilla with Cheese and Chile

Mexico's version of a grilled cheese sandwich makes a satisfying appetizer for nearly any occasion. Be sure to offer dishes of fresh tomato salsa and fresh guacamole alongside for spooning onto the crisp wedges.

Preheat a broiler (griller). Place the chiles on a baking sheet, slip under the broiler, and broil, turning as necessary, until the skin blackens and blisters on all sides. Transfer to a cutting board, drape loosely with aluminum foil, and let cool for 10 minutes. Peel away the skin (it's okay if some black spots remain) then remove the stems and seeds. Cut the chiles into small dice.

Heat 1 or 2 large frying pans over medium-high heat. Add $1/2$ tablespoon of the oil and swirl to coat the bottom of the pan(s). When the oil is very hot but not smoking, add 1 of the flour tortillas. Immediately top with about $1/2$ cup of the cheese, spreading it evenly. Season with salt, then scatter some of the chiles, cilantro, and green onions evenly over the cheese.

When the cheese is mostly melted and the tortilla is nicely browned on the bottom, after 1 to 2 minutes, place one of the remaining tortillas on top. Using a long spatula, carefully and quickly turn the quesadilla over in the frying pan. Reduce the heat to medium. Cook on the second side until the bottom is nicely browned, 1–2 minutes longer. Remove from the pan and keep warm. Repeat with the remaining tortillas and filling. (Alternatively, cook several quesadillas at once on an oiled griddle.)

Transfer the warm quesadillas to a cutting board and cut into wedges. Serve hot.

Serves 6 –8

2 or 3 Anaheim or poblano chiles

2 tablespoons vegetable oil

8 flour tortillas, each about 8 inches (20 cm) in diameter

$1/2$ pound (8 oz/250 g) Monterey jack cheese, shredded

salt to taste

$1/2$ cup ($3/4$ oz/20 g) coarsely chopped fresh cilantro

4 green onions, white and pale green parts only, minced

Oven-Fried Green Tomatoes with Lemon Cream

Green tomatoes are available from the summer months into Autumn in farmers' markets and at some specialty stores. Halved green cherry tomatoes can be baked and topped in the same manner. Garnish with additional strips of lemon zest, if desired.

¼ cup (1 oz/30 g) fine dried bread crumbs

Olive oil as needed

¼ cup (1 oz/30 g) grated Parmesan cheese

¼ cup (1½ oz/45 g) yellow cornmeal

1 tablespoon minced fresh flat-leaf (Italian) parsley

2 teaspoons minced fresh thyme

Salt and ground pepper to taste

3 eggs

½ cup (2½ oz/75 g) all-purpose (plain) flour

1 lb (500 g) green (unripened) tomatoes, cut into slices ½ inch (12 mm) thick

1 cup (8 oz/250 g) part-skim ricotta cheese

1 teaspoon grated lemon zest

Preheat an oven to 350°F (180°C). Spread the bread crumbs in a small pan and toast in the oven until lightly browned, about 8 minutes. Transfer to a shallow bowl and let cool.

Reduce the oven temperature to 325°F (165°C). Coat a baking sheet with a thin layer of olive oil.

Add the Parmesan cheese, cornmeal, parsley, and thyme to the bread crumbs and stir to mix. Season with salt and pepper. In another bowl, beat the eggs until blended. Place the flour in a third bowl.

One at a time, dip the tomato slices into the flour, lightly dusting both sides. Then dip into the eggs and immediately into the crumb mixture, coating both sides well. Place slightly apart on the prepared baking sheet.

Bake until golden brown on top, about 15 minutes. Remove from the oven and turn over the slices with a spatula. Return to the oven until golden brown on the second side, about 10 minutes longer.

Meanwhile, place the ricotta in a bowl and, using an electric mixer, whip until light and smooth. Mix in the lemon zest and season lightly with salt and pepper.

Transfer the tomatoes to a warmed platter and top each slice with a dollop of the ricotta cream. Serve warm.

Serves 6

Savory Vegetable Fritters

One bite will confirm why these deep-fried fritters, called *pakora*, are one of India's most popular afternoon snacks. They are delicious served on their own, but can also be accompanied with a fruit chutney such as tamarind or ginger.

To make the batter, in a bowl, combine the 1½ cups (6 oz/185 g) flour, salt, garam masala, coriander, baking powder, turmeric, and chile. Add the lemon juice and slowly mix in ⅓ cup (3 fl oz/80 ml) of the water, stirring to remove any lumps. Add only enough additional water, 1 tablespoon at a time, until the mixture is the consistency of a thick cake batter. Cover and let stand for 10 minutes.

In a large bowl, toss together the yam, broccoli, eggplant, spinach, and bell pepper. You should have 3½ cups (17½ oz/545 g) vegetables; do not use more than this amount. Again, adjust the batter by adding flour or water, until it is the consistency of a thick cake batter. Add the vegetables to the batter and stir thoroughly to combine. The vegetables should hold together when scooped up with a tablespoon.

In a large, deep frying pan over medium-high heat, pour oil to a depth of 2 inches (5 cm) and heat until 360°F (182°C) on a deep-frying thermometer. Working in batches, carefully drop the mixture, 1 tablespoon at a time, into the oil, without crowding. Fry until golden brown, about 3 minutes. Using a slotted spoon, transfer the fritters to paper towels to drain.

Serve hot or at room temperature.

Serves 6–8

1½ cups (6 oz/185 g) sifted chickpea (garbanzo bean) flour, or more as needed

1½ teaspoons salt

1 teaspoon garam masala (see glossary, page 293)

1 teaspoon ground coriander

1 teaspoon baking powder

¼ teaspoon turmeric

1 green chile, seeded and finely chopped

1 tablespoon lemon juice

⅔ cup (5 fl oz/160 ml) water, or more as needed

1 small yam, about 3 oz (90 g), peeled and cut into small dice

1 cup (2 oz/60 g) small broccoli florets

1 small Asian (slender) eggplant (aubergine), cut into small dice

6 spinach leaves, coarsely chopped

½ red bell pepper (capsicum), cut into small dice

Peanut or corn oil for frying

Baked Eggplant Rolls

These tender eggplant rolls have a savory stuffing of bell pepper, pecorino cheese, and bread crumbs. For tips on roasting bell peppers (capsicums) and making fresh bread crumbs, consult the glossary (page 292).

2 eggplants (aubergines), about 1 lb (500 g) each

1½ teaspoons salt, plus salt to taste

2 red bell peppers (capsicums), roasted, peeled, and finely chopped

¼ cup (1 oz/30 g) lightly toasted fine fresh bread crumbs

¾ cup (3 oz/90 g) grated pecorino cheese

1 tablespoon pine nuts

4 tablespoons (2 fl oz/60 ml) extra-virgin olive oil

2 cloves garlic, minced

Ground pepper to taste

About 16 fresh basil leaves, coarsely chopped

White wine vinegar to taste

1 tablespoon minced fresh flat-leaf (Italian) parsley

Cut the eggplants lengthwise into slices ⅓ inch (9 mm) thick. You should have 10–12 slices. Use only the 8 largest slices (reserve the others for another use). Arrange them on a rack. Using the 1½ teaspoons salt, sprinkle the tops of the slices. Let stand for 2 hours. The slices will exude moisture. Pat dry with paper towels.

Bring a large pot three-fourths full of salted water to a boil. Working in batches, add the eggplant slices and cook until supple enough to roll easily, 5–6 minutes. Using tongs, transfer to a kitchen towel to drain.

In a small bowl, combine the bell peppers, bread crumbs, ¼ cup (1 oz/30 g) of the pecorino cheese, pine nuts, and 1 tablespoon of the olive oil. Stir to mix well. In a small frying pan over medium-low heat, warm 1 tablespoon of the remaining olive oil. Add the garlic and sauté for 1 minute. Add to the bell pepper mixture. Season generously with salt and pepper.

Preheat an oven to 375°F (190°C). Oil a baking dish large enough to accommodate the eggplant rolls in a single layer. Arrange the eggplant slices on a work surface. Divide the bread crumb stuffing among the slices, spreading it in a thin layer. Scatter the basil evenly over the stuffing. Roll up each slice into a neat cylinder, then arrange, seam sides down, in the prepared dish. Drizzle the rolls evenly with the remaining 2 tablespoons olive oil, and sprinkle lightly with vinegar.

Bake until tender when pierced, about 1 hour. Remove from the oven and sprinkle with the remaining ½ cup (2 oz/60 g) pecorino cheese and the parsley. Serve hot.

Makes 8 rolls; serves 4

Fennel Frittata

Other vegetables such as roasted bell peppers (capsicums) or sautéed zucchini (courgettes) can be used instead of the fennel. The frittata can be cooked up to 1 day in advance, covered, and refrigerated. Bring to room temperature before serving.

Cut off the stems and feathery tops and any bruised outer stalks from the fennel bulbs. Dice the bulbs.

Preheat an oven to 400°F (200°C).

In a large frying pan over medium-low heat, warm 1 tablespoon of the olive oil. Add the fennel and cook, stirring occasionally, until almost soft, 12–15 minutes. Add the garlic, lemon zest, and lemon juice and stir together. Continue to cook, stirring, until the fennel is very soft, about 5 minutes. Season with salt and pepper. Remove from the heat and let cool slightly.

In a bowl, whisk together the eggs, milk, cheese, and parsley until frothy. Add the fennel and mix well. Season with salt and pepper.

In a 10-inch (25-cm) nonstick ovenproof frying pan over medium-high heat, warm the remaining 1 tablespoon olive oil. Add the egg mixture, reduce the heat to medium, and cook, occasionally loosening the edges with a spatula to allow the uncooked portion to run underneath, until the bottom of the frittata is set and the top is still runny, 7–8 minutes. Transfer to the oven and continue to cook until the eggs are set and the top is golden brown, 6–7 minutes.

Remove the frittata from the oven and loosen the bottom with a spatula. Invert a plate over the top of the frying pan. Holding them together firmly, flip the plate and pan so the frittata falls onto the plate.

Cut the frittata into wedges and serve hot, warm, or at room temperature.

Serves 6

2 small fennel bulbs

2 tablespoons olive oil

2 cloves garlic, minced

1/2 teaspoon grated lemon zest

1 tablespoon lemon juice

Salt and ground pepper to taste

8 eggs

3 tablespoons milk

1/2 cup (2 oz/60 g) grated pecorino or Parmesan cheese

2 tablespoons chopped fresh flat-leaf (Italian) parsley

Crispy Polenta Fingers with Tomato-Pepper Sauce

3 cups (24 fl oz/750 ml) water

1/2 teaspoon coarse salt, plus salt to taste

1/2 cup (3 oz/90 g) plus 2 tablespoons polenta

3 tablespoons grated Parmesan cheese

1 tablespoon unsalted butter, at room temperature

1 teaspoon chopped fresh rosemary

Ground black pepper to taste

FOR THE SAUCE

1 large red bell pepper (capsicum), roasted and peeled (see glossary, page 294)

2 tablespoons sour cream

1 tablespoon tomato paste

1/2 cup (4 fl oz/125 ml) heavy (double) cream

1 teaspoon balsamic vinegar

Pinch of cayenne pepper

Salt and ground black pepper to taste

1 1/2 cups (7 1/2 oz/235 g) all-purpose (plain) flour

Olive oil and safflower oil for deep-frying

Butter a 5-by-9-inch (13-by-23-cm) loaf pan. In a saucepan over high heat, bring the water to a boil. Add the 1/2 teaspoon salt, reduce the heat to medium, and slowly add the polenta, whisking constantly. Continue to whisk the mixture until it thickens, about 2 minutes. Change to a wooden spoon and continue to simmer, stirring periodically, until the polenta pulls away from the sides of the pan and the spoon can stand upright, unaided, in the polenta, 20–25 minutes. Add the cheese, butter, and rosemary and stir to mix well. Remove from the heat, season with salt and pepper, and pour into the prepared pan. Smooth the top with a rubber spatula, cover, and refrigerate until set, about 2 hours.

To make the sauce, place the roasted bell pepper in a blender along with the sour cream and tomato paste and blend until a smooth paste forms. Transfer to a bowl and add the heavy cream, vinegar, and cayenne. Whisk until the cream thickens slightly. Season with salt and black pepper. Cover and refrigerate until serving.

Run a knife around the polenta to loosen it from the pan. Invert the pan to unmold the polenta. Cut into slices 1/2 inch (12 mm) thick. Cut the slices into sticks 3 inches (7.5 cm) long by 1/2 inch (12 mm) wide. You should have about 30 sticks. Place the flour in a bowl and, in batches, dust the sticks lightly with the flour. In a large, deep frying pan or in a saucepan over medium-high heat, pour in equal parts olive oil and safflower oil to a depth of 1 inch (2.5 cm) and heat to 375°F (190°C) on a deep-frying thermometer. Add the polenta sticks, in batches, and fry, turning as needed, until golden on all sides, 1–2 minutes. Using a slotted spoon, transfer to paper towels to drain. Sprinkle with salt. Keep warm until all the sticks are cooked.

Serve warm with the sauce.

Makes about 30 sticks; serves 6–8

Spinach Tiropites

Common all over Greece, stuffed filo pastries make a memorable appetizer. Serve these pastries with a glass of ouzo over ice. They can be assembled up to 3 days in advance, covered, and refrigerated. Bake as directed just before serving.

Heat a large frying pan over medium-high heat. Add the spinach with only the rinsing water clinging to the leaves, cover, and cook until wilted, about 1 minute. Drain well on paper towels, then squeeze out as much of the remaining liquid as possible. Place in a large bowl and add the cheese, eggs, mint, and nutmeg. Stir well to combine. Season with salt and pepper.

Preheat an oven to 375°F (190°C).

Lightly butter a baking sheet. Cut the stack of filo sheets lengthwise into 3 equal strips. Remove 1 strip and cover the remaining filo with a slightly dampened kitchen towel to prevent it from drying out. Place the strip on a work surface and brush lightly with melted butter. Place another strip on top. Brush the second strip lightly with melted butter. Place a heaping teaspoonful of the filling about 1 inch (2.5 cm) in from the bottom of the strip. Fold the uncovered end over the filling on the diagonal to form a triangular shape. Bring the bottom of the triangle up against the straight edge. Continue folding in this manner until the tip of the strip is reached, forming a triangular pastry. Brush lightly with melted butter. Place on the prepared baking sheet. Repeat with the remaining filo and filling.

Bake until golden, about 15 minutes. Remove from the oven and transfer to a platter. Serve hot, warm, or at room temperature.

Makes 30 triangles; serves 6

1½ lb (750 g) spinach, tough stems removed, well rinsed, and coarsely chopped

1½ cups (7½ oz/235 g) crumbled feta cheese

½ cup (2 oz/60 g) grated kefalotiri, Parmesan, or pecorino cheese

4 eggs, lightly beaten

2 tablespoons chopped fresh mint

½ teaspoon ground nutmeg

Salt and ground pepper to taste

½ lb (250 g) filo dough (20 sheets), thawed if frozen

½ cup (4 oz/125 g) unsalted butter, melted and cooled

Soft-Shell Crabs with Chile Sauce

FOR THE CHILE SAUCE

4 cloves garlic

4 red jalapeño chiles, seeded

1 piece fresh ginger, about 1¹/₂ inches (4 cm), peeled

2–4 tablespoons water

2 tablespoons peanut oil

¹/₄ cup (2 fl oz/60 ml) tomato paste or tomato ketchup

1 tablespoon Sriracha sauce or sweet chile sauce

1 tablespoon soy sauce

1 tablespoon brown sugar

1 cup (8 fl oz/250 ml) chicken broth

1 tablespoon cornstarch (cornflour) mixed with 3 tablespoons water

1 tablespoon lime juice or red wine vinegar

1 extra-large egg

6 soft-shell crabs, about 4 oz (125 g) each, cleaned

¹/₄ cup (1 oz/30 g) cornstarch (cornflour)

3 tablespoons peanut oil

Salt and ground pepper to taste

Sliced green (spring) onions for garnish

To make the sauce, in a blender, combine the garlic, chiles, ginger, and just enough water to facilitate blending. Process until a smooth paste forms.

Warm a wok over medium heat. Add the oil, stir in the paste mixture, and cook until fragrant and creamy, about 1 minute. Stir in the tomato paste or ketchup, Sriracha or chile sauce, soy sauce, sugar, and broth. Add the cornstarch mixture and cook, stirring constantly, until the sauce thickens, about 30 seconds. Add the lime juice or vinegar. Crack the egg into the wok and cook, without stirring, until it begins to set, about 2 minutes. Fold the egg into the sauce; do not overmix. Specks of egg should peek through the sauce. Remove from the heat, cover, and keep warm.

Place each crab on its back and twist or cut off the small, triangular apron-shaped shell flap. Turn the crab, lift up the shell, and, using your fingers or kitchen scissors, remove and discard any gray gills. Using scissors, cut off the eyes and mouth. Scoop out the soft matter just inside this cut and discard. Rinse the crab and pat dry with paper towels.

Dust the crabs with the cornstarch, shaking off any excess. In a large frying pan over medium-high heat, warm the oil. Add the crabs and fry, turning once, until brown and crisp, about 3 minutes on each side. Season with salt and pepper.

Add the crabs to the chile sauce and turn to coat evenly. Transfer to serving plates, sprinkle with green onions, and serve.

Serves 2–3

Mussels with Feta and Tomatoes

This classic Greek *meze*, or appetizer, can be made with other shellfish such as clams, shrimp (prawns), or scallops. Serve with plenty of crusty bread and a small glass of ouzo for the perfect accompaniments.

2 tablespoons olive oil

1 small yellow onion, minced

2 cups (12 oz/375 g) peeled, seeded, and chopped tomatoes (fresh or canned)

1 cup (8 fl oz/250 ml) dry white wine

1/4 teaspoon dried oregano

Pinch of red pepper flakes

1 teaspoon red wine vinegar

2 lb (1 kg) mussels, well scrubbed and debearded

6 oz (185 g) feta cheese, crumbled

Salt and ground black pepper to taste

1 tablespoon coarsely chopped fresh flat-leaf (Italian) parsley

In a large frying pan over medium heat, warm the olive oil. Add the onion and cook, stirring occasionally, until soft, about 7 minutes. Raise the heat to high and add the tomatoes, wine, oregano, red pepper flakes, and vinegar. Stir well and bring to a boil. Reduce the heat to low and simmer uncovered, stirring occasionally, until thick, 20–30 minutes.

Add the mussels, discarding any that fail to close to the touch, cover, and cook until most of the mussels open, 2–3 minutes. Uncover and, using tongs, transfer the opened mussels to a bowl. Re-cover and continue to cook until all the mussels have opened, a minute or so longer. Transfer the additional opened mussels to the bowl and discard any that failed to open. Remove the pan from the heat.

When the mussels are just cool enough to handle, remove the meats from the shells and return them to the pan; discard the shells. Add the feta cheese to the pan as well and return the pan to medium heat. Bring to a gentle simmer and cook for 30 seconds, until the mussels are heated through and the cheese is softened. Season with salt and black pepper, sprinkle with parsley, and serve.

Serves 6

Saganaki

This Greek fried cheese appetizer takes its name from the pan in which it is traditionally cooked. Kefalotiri, a sheep's milk cheese with a dense texture and a marked tang, is traditionally used in this dish.

In a small frying pan, pour in olive oil to a depth of $1/4$ inch (6 mm) and place over medium-high heat. As soon as the surface of the oil ripples, reduce the heat to medium-low.

Meanwhile, fill a bowl three-fourths full of water and slip the cheese sticks into it. Place the flour in another bowl. Remove the cheese from the water and immediately place it in the flour, dusting both sides evenly. Do not tap off the excess flour.

Working in batches, slip the cheese into the hot oil in a single layer and fry, turning once with a fork, until golden and crispy, 1–2 minutes on each side. The sticks should be soft all the way through, but not melting. Using the fork, transfer to a warmed platter and, working quickly, repeat with the remaining cheese sticks.

Drizzle with the lemon juice and garnish with the lemon wedges and olives. Serve piping hot.

Serves 6

Olive oil for frying

$1/2$-lb (250-g) piece kefalotiri, Italian fontinella, Gruyère, or pecorino romano cheese, cut into sticks about $1/2$ inch (12 mm) thick

1 cup (5 oz/155 g) all-purpose (plain) flour

$1/4$ cup (2 fl oz/60 ml) lemon juice

6 lemon wedges

12 Kalamata olives

Shrimp and Saffron Pancakes

These simple little Andalusian pancakes are typically made with shrimp the size of a small thumbnail, a specialty of the region. Use the smallest shrimp you can find. Serve these pancakes as they do in Spain, with a glass of golden amontillado sherry.

In a small frying pan over low heat, warm the 2 tablespoons olive oil. Add the green onion, cover until soft, about 3 minutes. Remove from the heat and let cool slightly.

In a bowl, stir together the all-purpose flour, chickpea flour, baking powder, salt, and pepper. Add the shrimp, cooked green onion, chopped parsley, paprika, saffron, and water. Stir well. The batter should be the consistency of a very heavy (double) cream. Cover and let stand at room temperature for 1 hour or refrigerate for up to overnight.

In a large frying pan, pour in the olive oil to a depth of $^{1}/_{4}$ inch (6 mm) and place over medium-high heat. When the oil is hot, drop in 2 tablespoons batter for each pancake, spreading out each mound with the back of a spoon to form a cake about $2^{1}/_{2}$ inches (6 cm) in diameter. Do not crowd the pan. Fry, turning once, until golden, about 2 minutes on each side. Using a slotted spatula, transfer to paper towels to drain. Keep warm. Fry the remaining batter in the same way.

Arrange on a warmed platter and serve at once. Garnish with parsley sprigs, if desired.

Makes about 20 pancakes, serves 6

2 tablespoons olive oil, plus oil for frying

¼ cup (³/₄ oz/20 g) minced green (spring) onion, including tender green tops

¾ cup (4 oz/125 g) all-purpose (plain) flour

½ cup (2 oz/60g) chickpea (garbanzo bean) flour

½ teaspoon baking powder

½ teaspoon salt

½ teaspoon ground pepper

½ lb (250 g) small shrimp (prawns), peeled and finely chopped

3 tablespoons chopped fresh (Italian) flat-leaf parsley, plus sprigs for garnish (optional)

½ teaspoon sweet paprika

Large pinch of saffron threads

1½ cup (12 fl oz/375 ml) water

Salt-Roasted Mussels with Pimiento Dipping Sauce

Pimientos, late-maturing sweet peppers usually available in autumn and into winter, make an excellent dipping sauce for these hot shellfish. If unavailable, substitute thick, meaty red bell peppers (capsicums).

2 pimiento peppers

3 cloves garlic

1 tablespoon extra-virgin olive oil

1 teaspoon lemon juice

¼ teaspoon salt

¼ teaspoon ground pepper

2 tablespoons mayonnaise

Rock salt for roasting

1 lb (500 g) mussels, well scrubbed and debearded

Preheat broiler (griller).

To make the sauce, cut the pimientos in half lengthwise and remove the stems, seeds, and ribs. Place, cut sides down, on a baking sheet. Broil (grill) until the skins blacken and blister. Remove from the broiler, drape the peppers loosely with aluminum foil, and let cool for 10 minutes. Using your fingers or a small knife, peel away the skins.

Preheat an oven to 500°F (260°C)

In a small food processor or a blender, combine the garlic, olive oil, lemon juice, salt, and pepper. Process until smooth. Transfer the purée to a small bowl. Add the mayonnaise and stir until well blended. You should have about ¹/₂ cup (4 fl oz/125 ml). Set aside until serving. The flavors will intensify as the mixture stands.

In a heavy ovenproof frying pan or baking dish, make a bed of rock salt about 1¹/₂ inches (4 cm) deep. Place in the oven for 15 minutes to heat the salt thoroughly. Discard any mussels that do not close to the touch. Remove the pan or dish from the oven and arrange the mussels in a single layer on the salt. Return it to the oven and roast just until the mussels open, 5–7 minutes. Discard any that did not open.

Remove from the oven and transfer the mussels to a platter, or bring the pan or baking dish to the table. If you do the latter, be careful, as the baking is extremely hot. Divide the dipping sauce among small individual bowls and serve alongside.

Serves 4

Fried Cod with Garlic Sauce

In the kitchens of Greece, this popular garlic sauce—known as *skordalia*—has many variations. It is traditionally thickened with bread if you are poor, potatoes if you have a bit of money, and nuts if you are wealthy.

FOR THE GARLIC SAUCE

6 oz (185 g) coarse country bread, crusts removed

4 cups (32 fl oz/1 l) water

1/2 cup (2 oz/60 g) walnuts

2 tablespoons white wine vinegar, or as needed

1/2 cup (4 fl oz/125 ml) olive oil

3 tablespoons mayonnaise

3 large cloves garlic, minced

Salt and ground pepper to taste

2 1/4 cups (11 1/2 oz/360 g) all-purpose (plain) flour

1 teaspoon baking powder

1/4 teaspoon salt

1/4 teaspoon ground pepper

1 1/4 cups (10 fl oz/310 ml) beer, at room temperature, or as needed

Olive oil for deep-frying

2 lb (1 kg) rock cod or halibut fillets, cut into bite-sized pieces

Lemon wedges

To make the sauce, place the bread in a bowl and pour the water over it. Immediately remove the bread from the water and squeeze it to remove the excess moisture. Discard the water.

In a food processor or blender, process the walnuts almost to a paste. Add the soaked bread, 2 tablespoons vinegar, olive oil, mayonnaise, and garlic and purée to form a smooth paste. Season to taste with salt, pepper, and with more vinegar, if needed. Set aside.

In a bowl, whisk together 1 1/4 cups (6 1/2 oz/200 g) of the flour, the baking powder, salt, pepper, and 1 1/4 cups (10 fl oz/310 ml) beer. The batter should be the consistency of pourable pancake batter. Add more beer or some water, if necessary, to achieve the proper consistency.

In a deep, heavy saucepan, pour in olive oil to a depth of 2 inches (5 cm) and heat to 375°F (190°C) on a deep-frying thermometer. Meanwhile, place the remaining 1 cup (5 oz/160 g) flour in a bowl. Dust the fish pieces with the flour, coating evenly and tapping off the excess, then dip the fish into the batter. Add the fish to the oil, in batches, and fry until golden and crispy, 1–2 minutes. Using a slotted spoon, transfer to paper towels to drain. Keep warm until all the fish is cooked.

Transfer the fish to a warmed platter and garnish with lemon wedges. Serve the sauce alongside.

Serves 6

Shrimp and Jicama in Soy Sauce

Jicama has a delicate, crunchy texture and a mild flavor not unlike that of water chestnuts. Serve this dish as a first-course salad on a bed of mixed greens, or with toothpicks for a casually passed hors d'oeuvre.

In a small, dry frying pan over high heat, toasts the sesame seeds, stirring often, until lightly golden, about 2 minutes.

In a bowl, combine the soy sauce, sherry, cornstarch, ginger, sea salt, and dry mustard. Stir to mix well.

In a sauté pan over medium-high heat, warm the sesame oil. Add the shrimp, reduce the heat to medium, and cook, stirring, until the shrimp are opaque, about 2 minutes. Transfer the shrimp and any pan juices to the bowl holding the soy-sherry mixture and turn to coat the shrimp. Add the jicama and turn to coat as well.

Arrange the shrimp and jicama on 4 individual plates. Top with the sesame seeds and the cilantro and serve hot or warm.

Serves 4

¼ cup (³/₄ oz/20 g) sesame seeds

2 tablespoons soy sauce

1 tablespoon dry sherry

1 teaspoon cornstarch (cornflour)

½ teaspoon peeled and finely grated fresh ginger

¼ teaspoon sea salt

¼ teaspoon dry mustard

1 tablespoon Asian sesame oil

½ lb (250 g) shrimp (prawns), peeled and deveined

½ jicama, peeled and julienned

⅓ cup (¹/₃ oz/10g) chopped fresh cilantro (fresh coriander)

Crab Cakes with Sweet-and-Sour Cucumber Salad

In a large bowl, combine the pork, minced shallots, red serrano chile, green onion, bell pepper, 2 tablespoons of the cilantro, 2 tablespoons bread crumbs, fish sauce, pepper, $1/2$ teaspoon of the salt, $1/4$ teaspoon sugar, and egg. Mix well. If the mixture is too moist and does not hold together, add more panko or bread crumbs. Add the crabmeat and mix without compressing the crab.

Place the 1 cup (4 oz/125 g) panko or bread crumbs in a shallow dish. Scoop up $1/3$ cup (3 oz/90 g) crab mixture and form it into a cake 3 inches (7.5 cm) in diameter and $3/4$ inch (2 cm) thick. Dip each crab cake into the bread crumbs, pressing it into the crumbs and turning to coat both sides. Arrange on a baking sheet. You should have 8 cakes. Loosely cover with plastic wrap and refrigerate for 30 minutes.

Meanwhile, in a small saucepan over medium-high heat, combine the vinegar, 2 tablespoons sugar, and remaining $1/2$ teaspoon salt and bring to a boil. Cook, stirring occasionally, until a light syrup forms, about 5 minutes. Let cool. Place the cucumber, green serrano chile, and sliced shallot in a nonaluminum bowl; add the vinegar mixture, stir gently, and let stand for 15 minutes. Divide the cucumber salad among 4 small plates. Just before serving, sprinkle evenly with the remaining 1 tablespoon cilantro and the peanuts.

In a large frying pan over medium-high heat, pour oil to a depth of $1/4$ inch (6 mm) and heat until 360°F (182°C) on a deep-frying thermometer. Add the crab cakes without crowding them in the pan and fry, turning once, until crisp and golden brown, 2–3 minutes on each side. Using a slotted spatula, transfer to paper towels to drain.

Serve hot with the cucumber salad.

Makes 8 cakes; serves 4

1/2 lb (250 g) ground (minced) pork butt

2 shallots, finely minced, plus 1 large shallot, finely sliced

1 red serrano chile, minced

1 green (spring) onion, finely sliced

1/4 cup (1 oz/30 g) finely diced red bell pepper (capsicum)

3 tablespoons coarsely chopped fresh cilantro (fresh coriander)

2 tablespoons fine dried white bread crumbs, plus 1 cup (4 oz/125 g) for coating

1 tablespoon fish sauce

1 teaspoon ground pepper

1 teaspoon salt

1/4 teaspoon plus 2 tablespoons sugar

1 egg, lightly beaten

1/2 lb (250 g) cooked fresh crabmeat, flaked

1/2 cup (4 fl oz/125 ml) rice vinegar

1/2 English (hothouse) cucumber, peeled, quartered lengthwise, and thinly sliced

1 green serrano chile, minced

2 tablespoons chopped roasted peanuts

Peanut oil or corn oil for frying

Fried Oysters with Tartar Sauce

A glass of sparkling wine is the perfect pairing for the toasty crunch and sprinkling of salt on these delectable oysters. This dish is at its best when you shuck the oysters just before cooking to keep them moist.

FOR THE TARTAR SAUCE

3/4 cup (6 fl oz/180 ml) mayonnaise

3 tablespoons finely minced white onion

2 tablespoons *each* minced fresh chives and chopped fresh flat-leaf (Italian) parsley

2 tablespoons minced cornichons, plus brine from jar, if needed

1 tablespoon *each* chopped capers, Dijon mustard, and lemon juice

Salt and ground pepper to taste

24 oysters in the shell

Peanut oil for deep-frying

3 eggs

3 tablespoons whole milk

1 cup (5 oz/155 g) all-purpose (plain) flour, or as needed

Salt and ground pepper to taste

1 cup (4 oz/125 g) fine cracker crumbs, or as needed

To make the tartar sauce, in a bowl, combine the mayonnaise, white onion, chives, parsley, cornichons, capers, mustard, and lemon juice. Season with salt and pepper. Taste and adjust with liquid from the cornichons if more tartness is desired. Cover and refrigerate until needed.

Grip each oyster, flat side up, with a folded kitchen towel. To one side of the hinge, push in the tip of an oyster knife and pry upward to open the shell. Run the knife blade all around the oyster to cut the muscle that holds the shell halves together. Discard the top shell. Run the knife underneath the oyster to cut its flesh free from the bottom shell, then discard the bottom shell.

Line a baking sheet with parchment (baking) or waxed paper. Pour oil into a heavy sauté pan or cast-iron frying pan to a depth of 2 inches (5 cm) and heat to 375°F (190°C) on a deep-frying thermometer, or until the surface of the oil ripples.

Meanwhile, in a small bowl, whisk together the eggs and milk. Spread the flour on a plate and season lightly with salt and pepper. Spread the cracker crumbs on another plate. Dip each oyster in the flour, coating evenly, then in the egg mixture, then in the cracker crumbs. Set aside on the lined baking sheet until all are coated.

Slip the oysters into the hot oil, a few at a time, and fry until golden, 1–2 minutes. Using a slotted spoon or wire skimmer, transfer to paper towels to drain briefly. Sprinkle with salt. Arrange the oysters on a warmed platter or individual plates and serve immediately with the tartar sauce.

Serves 4

Savory Zucchini Pancakes

These pancakes have a texture and flavor reminiscent of puréed squash. Choose zucchini with thin skins, as thick-skinned ones may have a bitter taste that will not sufficiently mellow during the brief cooking time.

Trim all the zucchini, but do not peel. Shred the zucchini, then the onion. In a bowl toss the shredded zucchini with the salt. Let stand for 5 minutes. Using your hands, squeeze the zucchini to remove excess liquid. Add the onion, egg, garlic, flour, marjoram, and pepper to the zucchini. Mix well.

Pour about 1 tablespoon vegetable oil into the bottom of a large frying pan to form a thin film, and place over medium-high heat. When the pan is hot, working in batches, drop in the squash mixture, using a heaping tablespoonful for each pancake. Using the back of a spoon, press on the top of each spoonful to form a pancake a scant $^{1}/_{2}$ inch (12 mm) thick. Fry until golden brown on the underside, 3–4 minutes. Turn and continue to fry until golden brown on the second side, 2–3 minutes longer. Transfer to a warmed platter and keep warm. Repeat until all the squash mixture is used, adding more oil to the pan as needed. Serve hot.

Makes about 12 pancakes; serves 4

2 yellow zucchini (courgettes)

4 green zucchini (courgettes)

$^{1}/_{2}$ yellow onion

$^{1}/_{2}$ teaspoon salt

1 egg, lightly beaten

2 cloves garlic, minced

1 tablespoon all-purpose (plain) flour

1 tablespoon chopped fresh marjoram

$^{1}/_{2}$ teaspoon ground pepper

1–2 tablespoons vegetable oil

Corn Cakes with Smoked Salmon

You can prepare the batter for these crisp corn cakes up to a few hours before cooking. Store it, covered, in the refrigerator until the oil is hot and ready for frying. The crème fraîche offers a wonderful richness to the finished dish.

1³/₄ cups (10¹/₂ oz/330 g) white or yellow corn kernels (from about 2 ears)

¹/₃ cup (2 oz/60 g) fine yellow cornmeal

¹/₃ cup (2 oz/60 g) unbleached all-purpose (plain) flour

¹/₂ cup (4 fl oz/125 ml) milk

¹/₄ cup (2 oz/60 g) unsalted butter, melted and cooled

2 eggs

¹/₂ teaspoon salt

¹/₄ teaspoon ground pepper

¹/₄ cup (2 fl oz/60 ml) melted clarified unsalted butter or peanut oil, or as needed

16 small slices smoked salmon

1 cup (8 fl oz/250 ml) crème fraîche

¹/₄ cup (¹/₃ oz/10 g) snipped fresh chives

Place the corn kernels in a food processor. Using on-off pulses, pulse only until a coarse purée forms. Do not overprocess. Transfer to a bowl and whisk in the cornmeal and flour until smoothly incorporated.

In another bowl, whisk together the milk, melted butter, and eggs until blended. Add to the corn mixture and stir to combine. Stir in the ¹/₂ teaspoon salt and ¹/₄ teaspoon pepper.

Place a large nonstick or well-seasoned sauté pan or griddle over medium-high heat. When hot, brush with the clarified butter or peanut oil. Using about 2 tablespoons batter for each cake, ladle the batter onto the hot surface and spread to form cakes about 3 inches (7.5 cm) in diameter. The batter should sizzle when it hits the pan. Cook until golden on the first side, about 3 minutes. Then turn and cook on the second side until golden and the center is set, about 2 minutes longer. Transfer to a plate and keep warm until all the cakes are cooked.

To serve, place 2 corn cakes on each warmed individual plate. Top each corn cake with 2 slices of smoked salmon, a generous drizzle of crème fraîche, and a sprinkling of chives. Serve immediately.

Serves 4

Chicken Satay with Peanut Sauce

This recipe calls for coconut milk and coconut cream, the rich layer of fat that rises to the top of canned coconut milk. Do not shake the can before opening. Spoon off the layer of cream for the marinade, then stir the remaining milk and use it in the sauce.

In a blender, combine 2 shallots, 2 garlic cloves, 1 chile, and 2 tablespoons of the lemongrass. Process until finely chopped. Add 1 tablespoon of the coriander, the granulated sugar, 1 teaspoon of the cumin, 1 teaspoon of the salt, and about 2 tablespoons water, just enough to facilitate blending. Process until a smooth paste is formed. Pour into a nonaluminum bowl, add the coconut cream, and mix thoroughly. Cut the chicken into 1-inch (2.5-cm) pieces and add it to the marinade. Stir gently, cover, and refrigerate for at least 4 hours or as long as overnight.

Prepare a fire in a grill. Position a rack about 2 inches (5 cm) from the heat source. If using wooden skewers, soak in water to cover for 20–30 minutes and drain.

In a blender, combine the galangal, remaining 3 shallots, remaining 3 cloves garlic, remaining 2 chiles, remaining 1 tablespoon lemongrass, remaining 1 tablespoon coriander, remaining 1 teaspoon cumin, and about 2 tablespoons water, just enough to facilitate blending. Process until a smooth paste is formed. In a saucepan over medium heat, warm the oil. Add the spice paste and cook, stirring occasionally, until fragrant, about 3 minutes. Add the peanut butter and cook for 2 minutes longer. Stir in the palm sugar, fish sauce, remaining 1/2 teaspoon salt, and 1/4 cup (2 fl oz/60 ml) coconut milk. Cook, stirring occasionally, until beads of oil appear on the surface, about 5 minutes. Stir in the lime juice. Add more coconut milk if needed to make a thick, creamy sauce. Pour into a shallow bowl.

Remove the chicken from the marinade, discarding the marinade. Thread 5 or 6 pieces on each skewer. Grill, turning once, until the chicken has charred edges, 8–10 minutes. Arrange the skewers on a serving platter. Serve with the peanut sauce.

Serves 6

5 shallots, quartered

5 cloves garlic, halved

3 red serrano chiles, halved

3 tablespoons finely chopped lemongrass, white part only

2 tablespoons ground coriander

2 teaspoons granulated sugar

2 teaspoons ground cumin

1 1/2 teaspoons salt

4 tablespoons water

2 tablespoons unsweetened coconut cream

8 boneless, skinless chicken thighs, about 1 1/2 lb (750 g)

1 piece galangal, about 1 inch (2.5 cm), chopped

2 tablespoons peanut oil

1/4 cup (2 1/2 oz/75 g) chunky peanut butter

1 teaspoon palm sugar

1 teaspoon fish sauce

About 1/4 cup (2 fl oz/60 ml) unsweetened coconut milk

1/4 cup (2 fl oz/60 ml) lime juice

Spicy Stuffed Omelet Pouches

This Southeast-asian specialty features a thin omelet enveloping a rich, tasty filling of chicken, green beans, tomatoes, and chile. Garnish each plate with a sprig of fresh cilantro (fresh coriander) and serve with Sriracha sauce or Thai fish sauce.

FOR THE FILLING

1 tablespoon peanut oil

3 cloves garlic, minced

1 small yellow onion, finely chopped

1 red serrano or jalapeño chile, seeded and chopped

1/2 lb (250 g) ground (minced) chicken

1/4 lb (125 g) green beans, trimmed and thinly sliced

2 tablespoons Thai fish sauce

1 tablespoon palm sugar or brown sugar

1/4 teaspoon ground pepper

1 tomato, coarsely chopped

1/3 cup (1/3 oz/10 g) coarsely chopped fresh cilantro (fresh coriander)

FOR THE OMELETS

4 eggs

2 tablespoons water

1 1/2 teaspoons Thai fish sauce

2 teaspoons peanut or corn oil

Preheat an oven to 250°F (120°C). To make the filling, in a wok over medium-high heat, warm the oil. Add the garlic, onion, and chile and toss and stir until the onion is golden, 2–3 minutes. Raise the heat to high, add the chicken, and toss and stir to break up any large clumps until the chicken is crumbled and dry, 3–5 minutes. Add the green beans, fish sauce, sugar, and pepper and toss and stir for 2 minutes longer. Add the tomato and toss and stir until the mixture thickens, about 3 minutes. Remove from the heat and stir in the cilantro. Transfer to a bowl and set aside.

To make the omelets, in a bowl, whisk the eggs, water, and fish sauce. In a 10-inch (25-cm) frying pan over medium-high heat, warm 1/2 teaspoon of the oil and swirl to coat the pan bottom. Pour in 1/3 cup (3 fl oz/80 ml) of the egg mixture, tilting the pan to spread it evenly over the pan bottom. Cook until brown and the edges begin to shrink from the pan sides, about 1 minute. Gently slip a spatula underneath the omelet, turn the omelet, and continue to cook until the second side is brown, about 30 seconds. Transfer to a flat surface, placing the well-browned side down.

Spoon 1/2 cup (4 oz/125 g) of the filling in the center. Fold 2 opposite sides so they overlap in the center. Fold in the remaining sides to enclose the filling and form a square. Transfer, seam side down, to a serving plate. Using a sharp knife, make 3 cuts at right angles in the top of the omelet to form a square, leaving 1 side uncut. Lift the square to expose the filling. Loosely cover the omelet with aluminum foil and keep warm in the oven until ready to serve. Repeat to make the 3 remaining omelet pouches. Serve immediately.

Serves 4

Empanaditas

These savory meat-filled Spanish turnovers can be formed, covered, and refrigerated up to 3 days in advance. Bake as directed. Or freeze for up to 1 month and bake them frozen, adding about 5 minutes to the baking time.

In a large frying pan over medium heat, warm the olive oil. Add the onion, bell peppers, and garlic and cook, stirring occasionally, until soft, about 10 minutes. Add the chorizo and veal and cook, stirring, until the veal is no longer pink, about 10 minutes. Add the tomatoes, olives, cumin, and saffron. Cover and simmer until all ingredients are heated through, about 10 minutes. Uncover and continue to cook until the moisture evaporates, about 5 minutes. Add the hard-boiled eggs and mix well. Season with salt and pepper.

Preheat an oven to 350°F (180°C).

Dust a work surface and a rolling pin with flour. Roll out the puff pastry $1/8$ inch (3 mm) thick. Using a round cookie cutter $3^{1}/2$ inches (9 cm) in diameter, cut out 24 rounds. Place about 1 tablespoon filling on one-half of each round. Brush the edges of half of the round with egg-water mixture. Fold each round in half, enclosing the filling and forming a half-moon. Press the edges together to seal. As the turnovers are formed, arrange them on an ungreased baking sheet.

Bake until golden brown, about 15 minutes. Serve hot or at room temperature.

Makes 24 turnovers, serves 6

2 tablespoons olive oil

1 yellow onion, minced

2 green bell peppers (capsicums) seeded and finely chopped

3 cloves garlic, minced

¼ lb (125 g) chorizo sausages, casings removed, filling diced

½ lb (250g) ground (minced) veal

1 cup (6 oz/185 g) peeled, seeded, or chopped tomatoes (fresh or canned)

¼ cup (1½ oz/45 g) Spanish brine-cured green olives, pitted and chopped

1 teaspoon ground cumin

Large pinch of saffron threads

2 hard-boiled eggs, peeled and finally chopped

Salt and ground pepper to taste

1 package (10 oz/315 g) frozen puff pastry sheets, thawed in the refrigerator

2 eggs lightly beaten with 1 tablespoon water

Turkish Flat Bread with Lamb and Tomatoes

FOR THE DOUGH

1/2 teaspoon active dry yeast

3/4 cup (6 fl oz/180 ml) warm water (115°F/46°C)

2 tablespoons olive oil

1 tablespoon unsalted butter, melted and cooled

2 1/4 cups (11 1/2 oz/360 g) bread (hard-wheat) flour

1/2 teaspoon salt

FOR THE TOPPING

3 tablespoons pine nuts

1 1/2 tablespoons olive oil

1 small yellow onion, minced

3/4 lb (375 g) ground (minced) lamb

3/4 cup (4 1/2 oz/140 g) peeled, seeded, chopped, and drained tomatoes

2 tablespoons tomato paste

1/4 cup (1/3 oz/10 g) chopped fresh flat-leaf (Italian) parsley

1/4 teaspoon *each* ground cinnamon and ground allspice

1/8 teaspoon ground cloves

1/2 teaspoon each salt and ground black pepper

1/4 teaspoon red pepper flakes

1 tablespoon lemon juice

2 tablespoons unsalted butter, melted and cooled

To make the dough, in a bowl, stir together the yeast and 1/4 cup (2 fl oz/60 ml) of the warm water. Let stand until foamy, about 10 minutes. Add the remaining 1/2 cup (4 fl oz/120 ml) warm water, the olive oil, butter, flour, and salt. Stir until the dough gathers together in a ball and pulls away from the sides of the bowl. Turn out onto a floured work surface and knead until smooth and elastic, 7–10 minutes. Place the dough in an oiled bowl, turning to coat with oil. Cover the bowl with plastic wrap and let the dough rise until doubled in bulk, about 1 hour.

Meanwhile, make the topping: In a small, dry frying pan over medium heat, toast the pine nuts, stirring constantly, until golden, about 1 minute. Transfer to a plate. In a large frying pan over medium-high heat, warm the olive oil. Add the onion and cook, stirring occasionally, until soft, about 7 minutes. Add the lamb, tomatoes, tomato paste, parsley, pine nuts, cinnamon, allspice, cloves, salt, black pepper, and red pepper flakes and cook slowly, breaking up the lamb with a wooden spoon, until the mixture is almost dry, about 8 minutes. Stir in the lemon juice. Let cool.

Preheat an oven to 500°F (260°C). Oil 2 baking sheets. Turn out the dough onto a floured work surface and divide into 12 equal pieces. Roll out 6 pieces into rounds 7–8 inches (18–20 cm) in diameter. Place 3 rounds on each prepared baking sheet and let rest for 10 minutes. Divide half of the filling evenly among the rounds, spreading it to the edges. It will not completely cover the dough. Drizzle evenly with half of the butter.

Bake until lightly golden around the edges but still soft enough to roll up, 5–7 minutes. (If your oven is too small to hold both baking sheets on the middle rack, bake in batches.) Remove from the oven and roll up each round into a cylinder. Serve immediately. Repeat with the remaining dough pieces and topping.

Makes 12 small flat breads; serves 6

Salads

Mixed Greens with Panfried Goat Cheese

You can buy everything you need for this salad at the farmers' market from early summer through autumn, the best time of the year for fresh goat cheese. The beets can be cooked, peeled, and diced up to 1 day in advance.

Trim off the greens from each beet, cutting to within $^1/_2$ inch (12 mm) of the crown. In a saucepan, combine the beets with water to cover by 2 inches (5 cm). Add $^1/_2$ teaspoon of the salt and bring to a boil over medium-high heat. Reduce the heat to low, cover, and simmer until tender, about 30 minutes. Remove the pan from the heat and drain. When cool enough to handle, peel the beets and cut into $^1/_4$-inch (6-mm) dice. Set aside.

Divide the cheese into 4 equal portions. Shape each portion into a round about 3 inches (7.5 cm) in diameter. (If you have purchased a log-shaped cheese, cut it into slices $^3/_4$ inch/2 cm thick.) In a bowl, mix the bread crumbs, thyme, pepper, and the remaining $^1/_4$ teaspoon salt. Pour the mixture onto a sheet of waxed paper. One at a time, press both sides of each cheese patty into the mixture. Set aside.

To make the vinaigrette, in the bottom of a large salad bowl, stir together the olive oil, vinegar, salt, and pepper with a fork.

Add the frisée, spinach, and the reserved beet greens to the salad bowl and toss to coat well. Divide among individual plates and set aside.

In a frying pan, warm the olive oil over medium heat. Add the cheese rounds and cook until lightly browned on the underside, 1–2 minutes. Turn and continue to cook until the cheese begins to spread slightly, about 1 minute longer. Slip a spatula under each patty and place it on a plate of dressed greens. Sprinkle with the diced beets and serve immediately.

Serves 4

5 or 6 small golden beets with greens intact, each about 1 inch (2.5 cm) in diameter

$^3/_4$ teaspoon salt

$^1/_4$ lb (125 g) fresh goat cheese

$^1/_2$ cup (2 oz/60 g) unseasoned medium-fine dried bread crumbs

$^1/_2$ teaspoon fresh thyme leaves

$^1/_2$ teaspoon ground pepper

FOR THE VINAIGRETTE

$^1/_3$ cup (3 fl oz/80 ml) extra-virgin olive oil

2 tablespoons red wine vinegar

$^1/_2$ teaspoon salt

$^1/_2$ teaspoon ground pepper

2 cups (2 oz/60 g) frisée leaves, interior pale yellow leaves only

2 cups (2 oz/60 g) baby spinach leaves

1 tablespoon extra-virgin olive oil

Celery, Mushroom, and Endive Salad

The creamy dressing that coats this salad mellows some of the sharpness of the endive. You can use hazelnuts (filberts) in place of the walnuts. Toast them as directed, then wrap the warm nuts in a towel and rub off the skins before chopping.

1 cup (4 oz/125 g) walnut halves

FOR THE DRESSING

½ cup (4 fl oz/125 ml) olive oil

¼ cup (2 fl oz/60 ml) walnut oil

¼ cup (2 fl oz/60 ml) lemon juice

¼ cup (2 fl oz/60 ml) heavy (double) cream

2 teaspoons Dijon mustard (optional)

Salt and ground pepper to taste

2 cups (8 oz/250 g) thinly sliced celery

2 cups (6 oz/185 g) thinly sliced cremini mushrooms

3 or 4 heads Belgian endive (chicory/witloof)

4–5 oz (125–155 g) Gruyère cheese, cut into strips

Preheat an oven to 350°F (180°C). Spread the walnuts on a baking sheet and place in the oven. Toast, stirring occasionally, until lightly colored and fragrant, 8–10 minutes. Remove from the oven and, when cool enough to handle, chop coarsely. Set aside.

To make the dressing, in a small bowl, whisk together the olive and walnut oils, lemon juice, cream, and the mustard, if using. Season with salt and pepper.

In a small bowl, combine the celery and mushrooms. Add about one-third of the dressing and toss to coat evenly.

Trim away the cores of the endives and separate the leaves. Place in a bowl, add about half of the remaining dressing, and toss to coat.

Divide the endive leaves among 6 plates. Top with the celery-mushroom mixture, again dividing evenly. Distribute the cheese strips evenly over the salads, top with the walnuts, drizzle with the remaining dressing, and serve.

Serves 6

Mesclun, Arugula, and Fennel Salad

A trio of taste sensations—sweet, sour, salty—and a host of exotic flavors come together in this salad. Mesclun, a mix of young, tender salad greens, is available from high-quality greengrocers.

In a small bowl, stir together the pear nectar and vinegar. Season with salt and pepper. Set the dressing aside.

Cut off the stems, feathery tops, and any bruised outer stalks from the fennel bulb. Cut the fennel bulb in half lengthwise and cut away and discard the core. Slice crosswise paper-thin. Set aside.

In a bowl, combine the mesclun and arugula. Add half of the dressing and toss well. Place the greens on individual plates, dividing them evenly. Top the greens with the fennel, prosciutto, and figs, and drizzle with the remaining dressing. Using a cheese plane or a vegetable peeler, shave thin slices from the cheese and sprinkle over the salads. Season with pepper and serve.

Serves 4

2/3 cup (5 fl oz/160 ml) pear nectar

1/4 cup (2 fl oz/60 ml) seasoned rice vinegar

Salt and ground pepper to taste

1 fennel bulb

5 oz (155 g) mesclun salad greens

1 cup (1 oz/30 g) arugula (rocket) leaves, torn into pieces

2 oz (60 g) thinly sliced prosciutto, julienned

4 figs, quartered through the stem end

1 oz (30 g) Parmesan cheese

Southwest Caesar Salad

Jicama, a sweet and crunchy tuber, plays the role of the croutons in this Tex-Mex variation of the classic salad. Mexican cotija, a dry part-skim milk cheese, replaces the usual Parmesan cheese. If unavailable, use a low-fat feta cheese instead.

¼ cup (2 fl oz/60 ml) lime juice

4 teaspoons olive oil

3 large cloves garlic, minced

1 tablespoon chili powder

2 teaspoons ground cumin

1½ teaspoons Worcestershire sauce

2 heads romaine (cos) lettuce, leaves separated, or 1 large head, leaves separated and torn into pieces

1 cup (4 oz/125 g) crumbled cotija cheese (see note)

1 jicama, ¾ lb (375 g), peeled and cut into ½-inch (12-mm) cubes

Ground pepper to taste

In a large bowl, combine the lime juice, olive oil, garlic, chili powder, cumin, and Worcestershire sauce. Stir to mix well.

Add the lettuce, cheese, and jicama and toss to combine and coat all the leaves. Season generously with pepper and serve.

Serves 6

Romaine, Gorgonzola, and Walnut Salad

Gorgonzola dolcelatte is the sweeter version of the fabulously rich, blue-veined cheese. If you cannot find it at your market, substitute Roquefort or a similar blue cheese. When in season, figs or grapes make a nice addition to the salad.

Preheat an oven to 350°F (180°C).

To make the walnut vinaigrette, in a bowl, whisk together the walnut and olive oils, balsamic and sherry vinegars, salt, and pepper. Set aside.

Spread the walnuts on a baking sheet and place in the oven. Toast, stirring occasionally, until lightly browned and fragrant, 8–10 minutes. Remove from the oven. Transfer to a small bowl, add 3 tablespoons of the vinaigrette, toss lightly, and let stand for 15 minutes before assembling the salad.

Place the torn romaine in a large bowl. Add the marinated walnuts and drizzle with the remaining vinaigrette. Toss well. Divide among chilled individual plates and top with the figs, grapes, or pears, if using, and the cheese, dividing all the ingredients evenly, and serve.

Serves 6

FOR THE WALNUT VINAIGRETTE

7 tablespoons (3½ fl oz/105 ml) walnut oil

2 tablespoons olive oil

2 tablespoons balsamic vinegar

1 tablespoon sherry vinegar

Salt and ground pepper to taste

1 cup (4 oz/125 g) walnuts, preferably halves

3 heads romaine (cos) lettuce, leaves separated and torn into bite-sized pieces

6 small ripe figs, quartered through stem ends (optional)

1 cup (6 oz/185 g) red or black seedless grapes, halved (optional)

2 small pears, quartered, cored, and thinly sliced (optional)

½–⅔ lb (250–315 g) Gorgonzola dolcelatte cheese, at room temperature, broken into bite-sized pieces

Salad of Young Fennel, Parmesan, and Mushrooms

Try making this Italian salad in early summer or autumn, when the first of the season's fennel—its flavor mild and true, its flesh crisp—appears in farmers' markets. Look for mushrooms that are very firm with caps tightly fastened to the stems.

1 young, tender fennel bulb

1/2 lb (250 g) firm fresh button mushrooms, brushed clean

3 tablespoons lemon juice

1 1/2 tablespoons extra-virgin olive oil

1 tablespoon chopped fresh flat-leaf (Italian) parsley

1/2 teaspoon salt

1/2 teaspoon ground pepper

8 large, attractive butter (Boston) lettuce leaves

Wedge Italian Parmesan cheese

Cut off the stems, feathery tops, and any bruised outer stalks from the fennel bulb. Using a mandoline or sharp knife, cut crosswise into paper-thin slices. You should have about 2 cups (8 oz/250 g). Place in a bowl.

Trim the stem from each mushroom to make a clean, flat surface, then cut the mushrooms into paper-thin slices. Add to the fennel along with the lemon juice, olive oil, parsley, salt, and pepper. Toss gently to coat evenly.

Divide the lettuce leaves evenly among 4 individual plates, making a bed on each plate. Then divide the fennel and mushroom mixture evenly among the plates. Using a vegetable peeler, cheese plane, or very sharp knife, shave 4 or 5 pieces of Parmesan from the cheese wedge directly onto each plate. You will need about 2 oz (60 g) total for the shavings. Serve at once.

Serves 4

Frisée and Spinach Salad with Pancetta

The success of this salad results from the balance it strikes among a variety of flavors: sweet and tangy from the balsamic vinegar, salty from the pancetta, and mildly bitter from the frisée. If frisée is unavailable, substitute chicory (curly endive), or radicchio.

In a small, nonstick frying pan over medium heat, cook the pancetta, stirring often, until crisp, about 5 minutes. Pour off all the drippings. Stir in the shallot and sauté until softened, 1–2 minutes. Remove from the heat.

In a small bowl, whisk together the oil, vinegar, and mustard. Season with salt and pepper.

Place the frisée and spinach in a bowl. Drizzle with the vinaigrette and toss well, then sprinkle with the pancetta-shallot mixture and toss again. Serve immediately.

Serves 4–6

1 oz (30 g) pancetta or other unsmoked bacon, minced

1/2 shallot, minced

1/3 cup (3 fl oz/80 ml) extra-virgin olive oil

2 tablespoons balsamic vinegar

1 teaspoon Dijon mustard

Salt and ground pepper to taste

1 head frisée, torn into bite-sized pieces

1/2 bunch young, tender spinach, about 6 oz (185 g), tough stems removed

Bresaola with Asparagus Salad

Save this antipasto for spring, when asparagus are at their best. If you can't find bresaola (cured air-dried beef), substitute prosciutto. Accompany this salad with thick slices of Italian bread, such as ciabatta or foccacia, if you like.

Ice water

1 lb (500 g) tender asparagus tips, thinly sliced on the diagonal (about 2 lb/1 kg before trimming)

3½ tablespoons extra-virgin olive oil

2 tablespoons minced fresh flat-leaf (Italian) parsley

1 large shallot, minced

1 clove garlic, minced

Salt and ground pepper to taste

Lemon juice to taste

¼ lb (125 g) bresaola, sliced paper-thin (see note)

Have ready a bowl of ice water. Bring a pot three-fourths full of salted water to a boil. Add the asparagus and boil until tender-crisp, about 2 minutes. Drain and transfer to the ice water to stop the cooking. When cool, drain and pat dry with paper towels. Transfer to a bowl and add 2½ tablespoons of the olive oil and the parsley, shallot, and garlic. Season with salt, pepper, and lemon juice. Turn to coat the asparagus with the dressing.

Divide the bresaola among individual plates, arranging the slices in a slightly overlapping ring. Put one-fourth of the asparagus salad in the center of each ring. Drizzle the bresaola lightly with the remaining 1 tablespoon olive oil and serve.

Serves 4

Roast Asparagus Salad with Chèvre

Pass hot, crust-seeded semolina or whole-grain bread at the table for mopping up extra dressing from the plate. The dressing can be made up to 2 weeks in advance and stored, covered, in a nonaluminum container in the refrigerator.

Preheat an oven to 400°F (200°C). Line a rimmed baking sheet with aluminum foil and brush with olive oil.

Snap off any tough ends from the asparagus spears and trim the break with a sharp knife. Using a vegetable peeler, and starting just below the tip, peel the skin off each spear, down to the end. Arrange the spears in a single layer on the prepared pan, season with salt and pepper, and drizzle with the extra-virgin olive oil. Roast until tender, 12–14 minutes. Transfer to a plate and set aside.

To make the dressing, in a small bowl, whisk together the lemon juice, extra-virgin olive oil, olive oil, and mustard. Stir in the chives, and season with pepper.

Spoon about 2 tablespoons of the dressing over the asparagus and let stand while tossing the salad.

In a large bowl, gently toss together the green onions and the salad greens. Add the tomatoes. Drizzle just enough of the dressing onto the salad for the greens to glisten, and toss again. (You may not need to use all of the dressing.) Immediately mound the salad in the center of large individual salad plates. Place a slice of chèvre on top of each mound of greens, and arrange asparagus spears around the perimeter of each plate, dividing them equally. Drizzle a few extra drops of the remaining dressing over the chèvre. Serve immediately.

Serves 6

1½ lb (750 g) asparagus

Coarse salt and ground pepper to taste

About ½ teaspoon extra-virgin olive oil

FOR THE DRESSING

2 tablespoons lemon juice

2 tablespoons extra-virgin olive oil

2 tablespoons olive oil

1 tablespoon Dijon mustard

3–4 tablespoons snipped fresh chives

Ground pepper to taste

6 green (spring) onions, including about 2 inches (5 cm) of green, chopped

7–8 cups (7–8 oz/220–250 g) mixed baby salad greens

2 cups (12 oz/375 g) cherry tomatoes, red or mixed red and yellow, stems removed

¼ lb (125 g) herbed chèvre, cut into 6 slices

Warm Mushroom Salad with Shallot Vinaigrette

Serve this salad of mixed mushrooms and fragrant herbs as a robust and earthy beginning to a cool-weather meal. Any assortment of fresh mushrooms will work well. Try fresh local mushrooms for the best flavor.

3 large shallots, chopped

3 tablespoons sherry vinegar

3/4 cup (6 fl oz/180 ml) chicken broth

Salt and ground pepper to taste

5 oz (155 g) assorted baby salad greens

3/4 cup (3/4 oz/20 g) assorted fresh herb leaves such as tarragon, chive, basil, and parsley, in any combination

2 teaspoons hazelnut oil

1 lb (500 g) assorted fresh mushrooms such as cremini, porcini, morel, chanterelle, shiitake, and oyster, in any combination, brushed clean and quartered

1 package (3 1/2 oz/105 g) enoki mushrooms, trimmed

In a small saucepan over high heat, combine 1/4 cup (1 oz/30 g) of the shallots, the vinegar, and the broth. Bring to a boil and boil until reduced to 3/4 cup (6 fl oz/180 ml), about 3 minutes. Season with salt and pepper and set aside.

In a bowl, toss together the salad greens, herb leaves, and hazelnut oil until all the leaves are evenly coated with the oil. Season with salt and pepper; set aside.

Heat a nonstick sauté pan over medium heat. Coat the pan with nonstick cooking spray. Add the remaining shallots and sauté until softened, about 1 minute. Add the heartier mushrooms such as cremini and porcini, and sauté until browned, about 5 minutes. Add the more delicate mushrooms such as morels, chanterelles, and shiitakes, and coat them with nonstick cooking spray. Season with salt and pepper. Sauté until all the mushrooms are just tender, about 3 minutes longer. If using oyster mushrooms, add them during the last minute or two of cooking. Pour in the shallot-vinegar mixture and deglaze the pan, stirring with a wooden spoon to remove any browned bits from the pan bottom.

Divide the greens among individual plates. Top with the warm mushrooms and their juices, dividing evenly. Garnish with the enoki mushrooms. Serve immediately.

Serves 4

Arugula and Fennel Salad with Shaved Parmesan

Nutty arugula and crisp, licorice-flavored fennel have a natural affinity that is highlighted in this salad with a brisk lemon dressing. If you like, omit the Parmesan and add segments from 2 navel or blood oranges.

Cut off the stems, feathery tops, and any bruised outer stalks from the fennel bulb. Halve the bulb lengthwise and cut away the core. Thinly slice the bulb crosswise and place in a large bowl with the arugula.

To make the dressing, in a small bowl, whisk together the olive oil, $1^{1}/_{2}$ tablespoons lemon juice, and shallot. Season with salt and pepper. Add the dressing to the arugula and fennel and toss to coat. Taste and adjust the seasonings, adding more lemon juice if needed.

Divide the salad among individual plates. Using a vegetable peeler, shave about 4 paper-thin slices of Parmesan cheese onto each salad.

Serves 6

1 fennel bulb

$^{1}/_{2}$ lb (250 g) young arugula (rocket), thick stems removed

FOR THE DRESSING

3 tablespoons extra-virgin olive oil

$1^{1}/_{2}$ tablespoons lemon juice, or more to taste

1 shallot, minced

Salt and ground pepper to taste

2 oz (60 g) Parmesan cheese

Fennel, Sprout, and Herb Salad

If you cannot easily find chervil, substitute parsley or another complementary herb such as tarragon. Use alfalfa sprouts in place of the assorted sprouts, if you like, although variety makes a more interesting salad.

2 fennel bulbs

2 cups (4 oz/125 g) assorted sprouts such as sunflower, radish, onion, and clover

1 bunch watercress, tough stems removed

1/4 cup (1/3 oz/10 g) fresh chervil leaves

1 bunch fresh chives, snipped

1 bunch radishes, trimmed and coarsely grated

1/4 cup (2 fl oz/60 ml) lemon juice

1/4 cup (2 fl oz/60 ml) champagne vinegar

3/4 cup (6 fl oz/180 ml) safflower oil

1 teaspoon grated lemon zest

Salt and ground white pepper to taste

Cut off the stems, feathery tops, and any bruised outer stalks from the fennel bulbs. Coarsely chop the bulbs and place in a bowl along with the sprouts, watercress, chervil, chives, and radishes. Toss to mix well.

In a small bowl, combine the lemon juice and vinegar. While whisking continuously, slowly drizzle in the safflower oil to form a vinaigrette. Stir in the lemon zest, and season with salt and white pepper.

Drizzle the vinaigrette over the fennel and herb mixture, tossing to mix well. Serve at room temperature.

Serves 6

Fuyu Persimmon and Napa Cabbage Salad

Be sure to choose the small, round Fuyu persimmons, which are sweet when still firm. The more elongated Hachiya persimmons develop their characteristic sugar-sweet flesh only when very soft and pulpy and are not commonly served raw.

In a small, dry frying pan over medium-low heat, toast the sesame seeds, stirring continuously, until lightly golden and fragrant, 2–3 minutes. Transfer to a small plate and set aside.

Cut out the tough core from the base of the cabbage, then thinly slice the leaves. Place in a bowl. Trim away the stems from the persimmons, cut into quarters, and discard any seeds. Cut the persimmons into long, thin strips about $1/4$ inch (6 mm) wide. Add to the bowl holding the cabbage and toss to mix.

In a small bowl, stir together the oil, vinegar or lemon juice, sugar, salt, and pepper. Pour over the cabbage-persimmon mixture and toss to coat well.

Divide the salad evenly among individual plates or bowls. Sprinkle with the toasted sesame seeds and serve immediately.

Serves 4

$1/4$ cup (1 oz/30 g) sesame seeds

$1/2$ medium head napa cabbage, about 1 lb (500 g)

2 Fuyu persimmons

2 tablespoons corn or other light vegetable oil

2 tablespoons white wine vinegar or $1^1/2$ tablespoons lemon juice

$1/2$ teaspoon sugar

$1/4$ teaspoon salt

$1/4$ teaspoon ground pepper

Beet and Walnut Salad with Raspberry Vinaigrette

Marinating the beets in the vinaigrette infuses them with flavor and intensifies the color of the dressing. You decide how much garlic flavor to impart to the dressing. Allow the crushed garlic to rest in the vinaigrette for 1 hour or as long as 12 hours.

3 beets, about ³/₄ lb (375 g) total weight

¹/₃ cup (3 fl oz/80 ml) extra-virgin olive oil

3 tablespoons raspberry vinegar

¹/₂ teaspoon dry mustard

Salt and ground pepper to taste

1 clove garlic, lightly crushed and stuck onto the end of a toothpick

¹/₂ cup (2 oz/60 g) walnuts

2 heads Bibb or butter (Boston) lettuce, torn into bite-sized pieces

2–3 oz (60–90 g) Roquefort or other blue cheese, crumbled (optional)

Trim the stems from the beets, leaving about ¹/₂ inch (12 mm) intact; do not peel. Place the beets in a small saucepan, add water to cover, and bring to a boil. Reduce the heat to low, cover, and simmer until tender, about 20 minutes. Drain and, when cool enough to handle, cut off the stem and root ends and peel off the skins. Cut the beets into julienne strips and place in a bowl.

Meanwhile, in a small bowl, whisk together the oil, vinegar, and mustard. Season with salt and pepper and add the garlic. Let stand for 30 minutes. (The dressing may be made to this point up to 12 hours in advance and refrigerated. Return to room temperature before continuing.)

Preheat an oven to 350°F (180°C). Spread the walnuts on a baking sheet and toast until lightly colored and fragrant, 10–15 minutes. Remove from the oven and let cool.

Remove the garlic from the dressing and discard. Pour the dressing over the beets and let stand for at least 1 hour at room temperature or for up to 2 days in the refrigerator. (If necessary, bring to room temperature before serving.)

Just before serving, place the lettuce in a bowl. Using a slotted spoon, remove the beets from the dressing and place in another bowl. Drizzle the dressing over the lettuce and toss well to coat. Divide among individual plates. Top with the beets and garnish with the walnuts and the cheese, if using.

Serves 4–6

Warm Spinach Salad with Bacon and Potatoes

On a night when you prefer to eat lightly, make spinach salad your main course, accompanied by a slice or two of crusty bread or a bakery roll. On another occasion, replace the spinach with young arugula (rocket).

Place the potatoes and eggs in a large pot with water to cover. Place over medium-high heat, bring to a simmer, and adjust the heat to maintain a gentle simmer. Using a slotted spoon, remove the eggs after 8 minutes and run under cold water until cool. Add salt to the water and continue cooking the potatoes until easily pierced with a knife, 10–12 minutes longer. Drain and let cool, then peel if desired. Halve each potato lengthwise and cut crosswise into slices $1/4$-inch thick. Peel the hard-boiled eggs and cut into quarters lengthwise.

In a bowl, combine the spinach and red onion. Add the sliced potato.

Put the bacon in a cold frying pan and place over medium heat. Cook until the bacon begins to crisp and has rendered much of its fat, 5–7 minutes. Remove the bacon with a slotted spoon and add to the salad. Remove the frying pan from the heat. Pour off nearly all the bacon fat from the pan and discard or reserve for another use. In the same warm frying pan, away from the heat, whisk in the vinegar and then the olive oil, scraping up any browned bits that cling to the bottom of the pan. Taste and season with salt and pepper. Add the dressing to the salad and toss well. If needed, drizzle in a bit more olive oil. Toss again, taste, and adjust the seasonings.

Transfer the salad to a large serving bowl or rimmed platter. Arrange the egg wedges around the edge and serve at once.

Serves 6

$1^{1}/2$ lbs (24 oz/750 g) red boiling potatoes (about 6 medium)

6 eggs

Salt to taste

$1^{1}/2$ lbs (24 oz/750 g) baby spinach leaves, tough stems removed

1 red (Spanish) onion, thinly sliced

12 slices bacon, cut crosswise into $1/2$-inch (12-mm) wide pieces

3 tablespoons sherry vinegar or red wine vinegar, or to taste

$1/2$ cup (4 fl oz/125 ml) olive oil, plus extra if needed

Ground pepper to taste

Baked Goat Cheese Salad with Tomato Bruschetta

A salad of warm goat cheese on greens dressed with a light vinaigrette has been a French classic for decades. Here, the eponymous salad receives Italian dimension with the addition of thick slices of garlic- and tomato-rubbed toasts.

½ cup (4 fl oz/125 ml) plus 2 tablespoons extra-virgin olive oil

2½ tablespoons red wine vinegar

3 shallots, minced

Salt and ground pepper to taste

1 lb (16 oz/500 g) fresh goat cheese, sliced and patted into six ½-inch (12-mm) thick rounds

1 large loaf coarse country bread, cut into ½-inch (12-mm) thick slices

6 large peeled garlic cloves, halved

6 ripe plum tomatoes, halved crosswise

1 lb (16 oz/500 g) mixed baby salad greens

Preheat an oven to 350°F (180°C).

In a medium bowl, whisk together the ½ cup olive oil, vinegar, shallots, salt, and pepper to form a vinaigrette. Set aside.

Put the remaining 2 tablespoons oil in a baking dish. Add the goat cheese rounds and turn to coat both sides with the oil. Bake until the cheese is very soft and just beginning to lose its shape, about 8 minutes. Keep warm.

Position a rack in a broiler (griller) 4–6 inches (10–15 cm) from the heat source and preheat the broiler. Arrange the bread slices in single layers on 2 or more baking sheets. Broil the bread slices, turning once, until lightly browned and toasted. (Alternatively, bread can be toasted on an indoor or outdoor grill.) While hot, rub one side of each bread slice well with a cut garlic clove. Holding the tomato halves cut-side down, rub them vigorously over the garlicky side of each bread slice until each slice is liberally covered with tomato pulp and juice. Drizzle each with about ¼ teaspoon of the vinaigrette.

In a large bowl, toss the greens with the remaining vinaigrette. Taste and adjust the seasonings. Divide salad among 6 dinner plates. Using a metal spatula, place the warm goat cheese on top of the greens. Grind a little black pepper over the cheese. Place 2 tomato toasts on each plate, and pass the rest at the table.

Serves 6

Fava Beans with Pecorino, Olive Oil, and Lemon

Peeling a batch of fava beans can seem like a daunting task, but the process is actually quite simple and the results are well worth the time. They can be peeled 1 day in advance, covered, and refrigerated. Bring to room temperature before serving.

Bring a large pot three-fourths full of water to a boil over high heat. Add the shelled fava beans, reduce the heat to medium, and simmer until the skins begin to soften, about 20 seconds. Drain and let cool.

To peel the beans, using a small knife, pierce the skin of each bean opposite the end where it was attached to the pod. The bean will slip easily from its skin. Discard the skins and set the beans aside.

In a bowl, whisk together the olive oil, lemon juice, garlic, parsley, and lemon zest. Season with salt and pepper. Add the fava beans and toss together. Using a vegetable peeler, cut the pecorino into thin shavings directly over the bowl. Toss the mixture gently.

Transfer to a platter and garnish with the lemon wedges. Serve immediately.

Serves 6

4 lb (2 kg) fresh fava (broad) beans, shelled

3 tablespoons extra-virgin olive oil

2 tablespoons lemon juice

1 clove garlic, minced

1 tablespoon chopped fresh flat-leaf (Italian) parsley

1/2 teaspoon grated lemon zest

Salt and ground pepper to taste

Wedge of pecorino cheese, about 3 oz (90 g)

6 lemon wedges

Country Salad

In Greece, this familiar salad often includes crisp green tomatoes, which are surprisingly sweet, instead of red ones. Cruets of fruity Greek olive oil and red wine vinegar are set out for diners to dress their own salads.

4 small, ripe tomatoes, about 1¼ lb (625 g) total weight, cut into 1–1½-inch (2.5–4-cm) pieces

1 small red (Spanish) onion, cut into 1-inch (2.5-cm) dice

1 red bell pepper (capsicum), seeded and cut into 1–1½-inch (2.5–4-cm) pieces

1 English (hothouse) cucumber, cut into 1-inch (2.5-cm) pieces

5 tablespoons (2½ fl oz/75 ml) extra-virgin olive oil

3 tablespoons red wine vinegar

Salt and ground pepper to taste

¾ lb (375 g) feta cheese

¾ cup (4 oz/125 g) Kalamata olives

1 teaspoon dried Greek oregano

Toss the tomatoes, onion, bell pepper, and cucumber together. Drizzle with the olive oil and vinegar. Season with salt and pepper. Crumble the feta evenly over the top. Scatter the olives on top and sprinkle the salad with the oregano. Transfer to individual bowls and serve immediately.

Serves 6

Three Bean and Corn Salad

Tart and hearty, this filling bean salad makes a colorful side salad. Cook each variety of bean separately to ensure optimum texture and to maintain the color.

Pick over each variety of bean and discard any misshapen beans or stones. Rinse each variety separately and drain. Place in separate bowls, add plenty of water to cover, and let soak for 3 hours.

Drain and place each variety in a saucepan with water to cover by 2 inches (5 cm). Bring to a boil, reduce the heat to low, and simmer, uncovered, until tender, about 45 minutes for red beans, about 50 minutes for cannellini or Great Northern, and about 60 minutes for black beans. Drain, rinse, and let cool. The cooking times will depend on the type and age of the beans.

Meanwhile, bring a small saucepan two-thirds full of water to a boil. Add the corn kernels and blanch for about 2 minutes. Drain, rinse with cold running water to halt the cooking, and drain again.

In a bowl, combine all the beans with the corn, green onions, and bell pepper. Mix well.

In a small bowl, whisk together the oil, salsa, vinegar to taste, garlic, and cumin. Season with salt and pepper. Pour over the bean mixture and stir to mix. Let stand for at least 30 minutes or for up to 2 hours to allow the flavors to blend.

Just before serving, garnish with the cilantro.

Serves 6–8

1/2 cup (3 1/2 oz/105 g) dried red beans such as kidney

1/2 cup (3 1/2 oz/105 g) dried cannellini or Great Northern beans

1/2 cup (3 1/2 oz/105 g) dried black beans

1 cup (6 oz/185 g) corn kernels (cut from about 2 ears)

3 green (spring) onions, chopped

1 whole red bell pepper (capsicum) or 1/2 *each* red bell pepper and green bell pepper, seeded and chopped

1/3 cup (3 fl oz/80 ml) canola or safflower oil

1/4 cup (2 fl oz/60 ml) tomato salsa

2–3 tablespoons cider vinegar

2 cloves garlic, minced

1/2 teaspoon ground cumin

Salt and ground pepper to taste

1/2 cup (2/3 oz/20 g) chopped fresh cilantro (fresh coriander)

Feta Salad with Cucumbers, Onions, and Mint

This recipe could not be easier: just crumble and chop, toss it all together, stir for
a second, and it is ready. Use the warm pita bread for scooping it up. This versatile
dish is perfect for a picnic or alongside grilled meats such as lamb or chicken.

½ lb (250 g) feta cheese

2–3 tablespoons lemon juice

1 tablespoon extra-virgin
olive oil

Salt and ground pepper
to taste

1 English (hothouse) cucumber,
peeled, halved, seeded, and
thickly sliced

¼ cup (2 oz/60 g) diced red
(Spanish) onion (¼-inch/6-
mm dice)

6 green (spring) onions, white
portion plus 2 inches (5 cm)
of tender green tops, thinly
sliced

3 tablespoons chopped fresh
mint, plus sprigs for garnish

2 tablespoons chopped fresh
parsley

2 tablespoons chopped fresh
dill, plus sprigs for garnish

3 pita bread rounds, heated
and cut into wedges

Crumble the feta into a bowl. Add the lemon juice to taste, olive oil, salt, and
pepper and toss together with a fork. Add the cucumber, red onion, green onions,
and the chopped mint, parsley, and dill. Toss together to mix well.

Transfer to a serving plate and garnish with dill and mint sprigs. Serve with the
pita wedges.

Serves 6

Green Bean and New Potato Salad with Salsa Verde

Italian salsa verde, or green sauce, is also good on cooked beets, carrots, and cauliflower. It will keep for about 1 week in the refrigerator. For a heartier salad, add cooked tuna or salmon fillet, or quartered hard-boiled eggs to the plate.

In a saucepan, combine the potatoes with lightly salted water to cover. Bring to a boil, reduce the heat to medium, and simmer, uncovered, until just tender enough to pierce with a fork, about 20 minutes. Drain, let cool, and cut into wedges.

Meanwhile, bring a saucepan three-fourths full of lightly salted water to a boil. Add the green beans, blanch for 3 minutes, and drain. Immediately immerse in cold water to halt the cooking, then drain and pat dry with a kitchen towel.

To make the salsa verde, in a bowl, combine the parsley, onion, capers, garlic, anchovies, and bread crumbs. Whisk in the olive oil, vinegar or lemon juice, salt, and pepper until blended.

Arrange the potatoes and green beans on a platter. Drizzle on the salsa verde and serve.

Serves 6

1 lb (500 g) small new potatoes

1 lb (500 g) small green beans

FOR THE SALSA VERDE

1½ cups (2¼ oz/67 g) finely chopped fresh flat-leaf (Italian) parsley

4–6 tablespoons very finely chopped white onion

¼ cup (2 oz/60 g) capers, rinsed and coarsely chopped

6 cloves garlic, finely minced

4–6 anchovy fillets in olive oil, drained and very finely chopped

⅓ cup (1½ oz/45 g) fine dried bread crumbs

1 cup (8 fl oz/250 ml) extra-virgin olive oil

¼ cup (2 fl oz/60 ml) red wine vinegar or lemon juice

Salt and ground pepper to taste

Fattoush

Throughout the Mediterranean, bread salads have long been a staple. This particular version is an excellent way to use up leftover pita bread. Use the best fresh ingredients and good-quality extra-virgin olive oil for the finest flavor.

2 pita bread rounds, each 3–4 days old

1 English (hothouse) cucumber, peeled, halved, seeded, and diced

Salt for sprinkling cucumbers, plus salt to taste

3 tomatoes, about 1¼ lb (625 g) total weight, seeded and diced

6 green (spring) onions, thinly sliced

1 green bell pepper (capsicum), seeded and diced

⅓ cup (½ oz/15 g) coarsely chopped fresh mint

¼ cup (⅓ oz/10 g) coarsely chopped fresh flat-leaf (Italian) parsley

¼ cup (⅓ oz/10 g) coarsely chopped fresh cilantro (fresh coriander)

Ground pepper to taste

2 large cloves garlic, minced

¼ cup (2 fl oz/60 ml) lemon juice

⅓ cup (3 fl oz/80 ml) olive oil

Preheat an oven to 375°F (190°C).

Split each pita bread into 2 rounds by separating it along the outside seam, then tear the rounds into 1-inch (2.5-cm) pieces. Spread the pieces out on a baking sheet. Bake until lightly golden and dry, 10–15 minutes. Remove from the oven and place in a bowl.

Meanwhile, spread the diced cucumber on paper towels in a single layer, salt lightly, and let drain for 15 minutes. Transfer to a colander, place under cold running water for a few seconds, and then pat dry with clean paper towels.

Add the cucumber, tomatoes, green onions, bell pepper, mint, parsley, and cilantro to the bread. Season with salt and pepper and toss well.

In a small bowl, whisk together the garlic, lemon juice, and olive oil. Season with salt and pepper. Drizzle over the vegetables and bread and toss well.

Transfer the salad to a platter and serve at once.

Serves 6

Cilantro, Cucumber, and Red Chile Salad

With its hints of both Southwestern and Asian flavors, this salad makes a good accompaniment to roasted or grilled meats or poultry. It can also be tossed with mixed greens and cooked shrimp (prawns) and served as a main-course salad.

In a nonaluminum bowl, combine the cucumber and cilantro, then crumble in the dried chile. Sprinkle with the salt and add the vinegar and oil. Turn to coat well.

Let stand for 30 minutes to allow the flavors to blend. Serve at room temperature.

Serves 4

2 cucumbers, peeled and thinly sliced

1 cup (1¹/₂ oz/45 g) coarsely chopped fresh cilantro (fresh coriander)

3 small dried red chiles such as árbol, bird's-eye, or pequín, seeded

¹/₂ teaspoon salt

¹/₄ cup (2 fl oz/60 m) unseasoned rice vinegar

2 tablespoons canola, sunflower, or other light oil

Pasta Salad with Oranges, Fennel, and Watercress

Ideal for serving in the cooler months when oranges and fennel are at their best, this hearty salad can be partnered with soup for lunch or supper or set out as a side dish on a buffet. The recipe can easily be increased for larger gatherings.

FOR THE DRESSING

1/4 cup (2 fl oz/60 ml) plus 1 1/2 teaspoons orange juice

1/4 cup (2 fl oz/60 ml) plus 1 1/2 teaspoons white wine vinegar

1 tablespoon grated orange zest

3/4 teaspoon salt

Ground pepper to taste

3 tablespoons olive oil

FOR THE SALAD

1 lb (500 g) penne or other tube-shaped dried pasta

2 fennel bulbs

24 brine-cured black olives such as Kalamata, pitted and slivered

1/2 lb (250 g) feta cheese, crumbled

2 navel oranges

1 bunch watercress, tough stems removed (about 3 cups/3 oz/90 g tender leaves and stems)

To make dressing, in a small bowl whisk together the orange juice, vinegar, orange zest, salt and a few grinds of pepper. Whisk in the olive oil. (The dressing can be made up to 2 hours ahead of time. Cover and let stand at cool room temperature.)

To make the salad, bring a large saucepan three-fourths full of salted water to boil. Add the pasta, stir well, and cook until al dente (tender, yet still firm to the bite), about 12 minutes or according to package directions. Drain well, rinse with cold water until cool, and drain well again. Transfer to a large bowl.

Working with 1 fennel bulb at a time, cut off the stems, feathery tops, and any bruised outer stalks. Halve lengthwise, cut away the tough core portion, and cut into narrow julienne strips. Add to the pasta along with the olives and cheese. Toss well to combine. Whisk the dressing and pour half of it over the pasta. Stir to coat well. Let stand for 5 minutes or for up to 1 hour at cool temperature.

Working with 1 orange at a time and using a small, sharp knife, cut a slice off the top and bottom to expose the fruit. Place upright on the cutting board and thickly slice off the peel in strips, cutting around the contour of the orange to expose the flesh. Holding the orange over a bowl, cut along either side of each section to free it from the membrane, letting the section drop into the bowl.

Just before serving, add the orange sections, watercress, and the remaining dressing to the pasta mixture. Mix gently. Taste and adjust the seasonings, then serve.

Serves 6

Warm Shrimp and Haricots Verts Salad

You can cook the haricots verts up to 1 day in advance. Under-cook them slightly, drain, trim, and refrigerate. Just before serving, reheat the beans, tossing and stirring, in the hot dressing in the frying pan. Arrange on the lettuce and serve immediately.

In a nonaluminum dish, combine the shrimp, garlic, thyme, red pepper flakes, half of the lemon juice, and 4 tablespoons (2 fl oz/60 ml) of the olive oil. Toss well. Cover and refrigerate for at least 30 minutes or for up to 1 hour.

Meanwhile, bring a large saucepan three-fourths full of salted water to a boil. Add the beans and boil until barely tender, about 2 minutes. Drain and immediately plunge into very cold water to stop the cooking. Drain again and trim off the stem ends; leave the tiny tips of the beans intact. Set aside.

Preheat an oven to 450°F (230°C). Sprinkle a rimmed baking sheet with coarse salt. Remove the shrimp from the marinade, reserving the marinade, and arrange in a single layer on the prepared pan. Roast until they turn pink, begin to curl, and are tender, 7–8 minutes.

Meanwhile, in a large frying pan over high heat, bring the marinade to a boil. Cook for 3–4 minutes. Stir in the sun-dried tomatoes and the parsley. Add the remaining 2 tablespoons olive oil and as much of the remaining lemon juice as needed to create enough dressing for the salad, about 1/2 cup (4 fl oz/125 ml) total. Season with salt and pepper. Spoon 2–3 tablespoons of the warm dressing over the beans to reheat and toss to coat.

Line individual salad plates with the lettuce leaves. Divide the warm beans evenly among the plates, top equally with the shrimp, and drizzle about 1 tablespoon warm dressing over each salad. Garnish with the chives and serve immediately.

Serves 8

1½ lb (750 g) shrimp (prawns), peeled and deveined

2 large cloves garlic, minced

1 teaspoon dried thyme

1/2 teaspoon red pepper flakes

Juice of 2 lemons

About 6 tablespoons (3 fl oz/90 ml) olive oil

2½ lb (1.25 kg) haricots verts or young, tender green beans

coarse salt for roasting, plus extra to taste

8–12 oil-packed sun-dried tomatoes, drained and slivered

1/3 cup (1/2 oz/15 g) chopped fresh flat-leaf (Italian) parsley

Ground pepper to taste

8 large red-leaf lettuce leaves

1 small bunch fresh chives, snipped

Curried Crab Salad with Mango-Mojo Sauce

Lime juice, garlic, oregano, and cumin are some of the seasonings often found in the archetypal Cuban spiced vinaigrette known as *mojo*. Those same flavors, combined with a purée of fresh mango, give this sophisticated seafood salad a refreshing kick.

1 lb (500 g) asparagus, tough ends removed

1 mango, peeled, pitted, and sliced

1 tablespoon lime juice

1 small clove garlic, chopped

3/4 teaspoon ground cumin

1/4 cup (2 fl oz/60 ml) water, if needed

1/2 lb (250 g) fresh-cooked crabmeat, broken into pieces

1 cup (5 oz/155 g) peeled, seeded, and chopped cucumber

1/3 cup (3 fl oz/80 ml) fat-free mayonnaise

1/4 cup (1/3 oz/10 g) snipped fresh chives, plus extra for garnish, if desired

1 1/2 teaspoons curry powder

Salt and ground pepper to taste

Bring a saucepan three-fourths full of water to a boil. Add the asparagus and boil for 3 minutes. Drain and immerse in cold water to stop the cooking. Drain again. Cut all but 8 of the asparagus on the diagonal into 3/4-inch (2-cm) lengths. Set aside.

In a blender, combine the mango, lime juice, garlic, and cumin. Blend until smooth. If the mixture is too thick, thin to a sauce consistency with the water. Set aside.

In a bowl, combine the cut asparagus, crabmeat, cucumber, mayonnaise, 1/4 cup (1/3 oz/10 g) chives, and curry powder. Mix well and season to taste with salt and pepper.

Arrange the crab salad on a plate. Garnish with the reserved asparagus slices and a sprinkling of chives and serve. Pass the sauce at the table.

Serves 4

Salmon Salad with Beets

You can expand on this seafood salad with a few blanched green beans, steamed potatoes, or sliced tomatoes. The yogurt-cucumber dressing, similar to the Greek sauce *tzatziki*, is a delicious addition.

12 small red or golden beets

2 cups (16 fl oz/500 ml) water

2 tablespoons olive oil

6 skinless salmon fillets (about 6 oz/185 g each)

salt and ground pepper to taste

1 cup (8 fl oz/250 ml) dry white wine

FOR THE DRESSING

1¹/₂ cups (12 oz/375 g) plain yogurt

2 tablespoons olive oil

3 garlic cloves, minced

¹/₃ cup (¹/₂ oz/10 g) minced fresh dill

¹/₃ cup (1 oz/30 g) minced green onions, white and pale green parts only

1 cucumber, peeled, seeded, and grated

Salt and ground pepper to taste

3 heads butter (Boston) lettuce (about 1 lb total)

Preheat an oven to 400° F (200° C).

Trim off the beet greens, leaving ¹/₂ inch of the stem intact, and reserve for another use. Rinse the beets thoroughly, but do not peel. Place in a baking dish and add the water. Cover tightly and bake until tender when pierced, 45–55 minutes. Remove from the oven, keep covered, and let cool. (Letting the beets cool while still covered makes them easier to peel). Slip off the skins from the beets with your fingers or a small knife. Cut in half, then slice or cut into thick wedges. Set aside.

Reduce the oven temperature to 350° F (180° C). Put the olive oil in a baking dish, add the salmon, and turn to coat with the oil. Season with salt and pepper. Drizzle the wine around the fish. Bake until the salmon is just barely opaque throughout or until cooked to desired doneness, 10–15 minutes.

Meanwhile, make the dressing: In a bowl, whisk together the yogurt, olive oil, garlic, dill, and green onion. Stir in the cucumber. Season to taste with salt and ground pepper.

Clean and trim the lettuce heads, discarding the tough outer leaves. Separate the remaining leaves from the heads and line 6 dinner plates with the lettuce leaves. Remove the salmon fillets from the oven and place one in the center of each plate. Scatter the beet slices over the lettuce. Spoon a little of the dressing over the salmon. Pass the remaining dressing at the table.

Serves 6

Warm Shrimp and White Bean Salad

Bright pink-and-white butterflied shrimp look beautiful against a background of plump white beans. Use dried beans that are less than a year old, or they will not cook evenly.

Pick over the beans and discard any misshapen beans or impurities. Rinse the beans and drain. Place in a bowl, add plenty of water to cover, and let soak for 8 hours.

Drain the beans and place in a saucepan with the water. Add the yellow onion and rosemary. Bring to a simmer over medium heat, skimming off any foam. Cover partially, adjust the heat to maintain a gentle simmer, and cook until the beans are tender, about 1 hour. Remove from the heat and remove the onion and woody rosemary sprig (leave any detached leaves). Season the beans generously with salt and pepper. Keep warm.

Bring a large pot three-fourths full of salted water to a boil. Meanwhile, using a small knife, make a deep slit along the back of each peeled shrimp so it will open like a butterfly when cooked. With the tip of the knife or your fingers, lift up and pull out the long, veinlike intestinal tract. Add the shrimp to the boiling water and cook just until they turn pink, about 45 seconds; do not overcook. Drain and transfer to a large, shallow serving bowl.

Drain the warm beans and add to the bowl along with the olive oil, red onion, parsley, garlic, and vinegar. Toss well. Taste and adjust the seasonings. Serve at once.

Serves 6

1¹/₈ cups (8 oz/250 g) dried large white beans

6 cups (48 fl oz/1.5 l) water

¹/₂ yellow onion

1 fresh rosemary sprig, 4 inches (10 cm) long

Salt and ground pepper to taste

18 large shrimp (prawns), peeled

¹/₃ cup (3 fl oz/80 ml) extra-virgin olive oil

¹/₃ cup (2 oz/60 g) minced red (Spanish) onion

¹/₄ cup (¹/₃ oz/10 g) minced fresh flat-leaf (Italian) parsley

2 cloves garlic, minced

1 tablespoon red wine vinegar

Tomato and Tuna Salad

In summer, a cool, fresh salad of ripe tomatoes, hard-boiled eggs, and tuna makes an easy start to a pasta dinner. If you can find it, use good-quality Italian tuna packed in olive oil.

In a bowl, combine the tomatoes, tuna, olive oil, onion, capers, and garlic. Toss to mix. Season to taste with salt and vinegar and toss again. Just before serving, stir in the basil.

Arrange 2 or 3 lettuce leaves on each plate. Top each lettuce bed with one-fourth of the tomato-tuna mixture. Surround with the hard-boiled egg wedges and olives, dividing them evenly. Serve at once.

Serves 4

2 large tomatoes, seeded and chopped

1/2 lb (250 g) good-quality canned tuna (see note), drained and separated into large flakes

1/4 cup (2 fl oz/60 ml) extra-virgin olive oil

1/4 cup (1 1/2 oz/45 g) minced red (Spanish) onion

2 teaspoons capers

2 cloves garlic, minced

Salt to taste

White wine vinegar to taste

About 12 fresh basil leaves, torn into small pieces

1 heart butter (Boston) lettuce, separated into leaves

2 hard-boiled eggs, peeled and quartered lengthwise

12 Mediterranean-style oil-cured black olives

Pan-Seared Salmon with Pea Shoots and Watercress

Once cooked, the salmon and its pan juices become a topping for a tangle of sprightly flavored greens dressed with a lemon vinaigrette. Pea shoots, the clippings from young pea plants, have a mild pealike flavor that blends well with the other greens.

2/3 cup (5 fl oz/160 ml) extra-virgin olive oil

1/3 cup (3 fl oz/80 ml) lemon juice, preferably from Meyer lemons

3 shallots, minced

1/2 teaspoon salt

1/2 teaspoon ground pepper

1/4 teaspoon sugar, if needed

5 cups (5 oz/155 g) watercress leaves

5 cups (5 oz/155 g) pea shoots, arugula (rocket) leaves, or mixed baby greens

FOR THE SALMON

1 1/2 teaspoon salt

8 salmon fillets, each about 1/3 lb (5 oz/155g) and 1/2 inch (12 mm) thick

1 teaspoon ground pepper

1/2 cup (4 fl oz/125 ml) *each* dry white wine and lemon juice, preferably from meyer lemons

4 tablespoons (2 fl oz/60 ml) water

In a large bowl, combine the olive oil, lemon juice, shallots, salt, and pepper. Add the sugar if not using juice from Meyer lemons. Mix until well blended.

Add the watercress leaves and pea shoots to the dressing and turn gently to coat well. Divide the greens evenly among 8 individual plates.

To prepare the salmon, sprinkle the salt in a wide, heavy frying pan and place on medium-high heat until nearly smoking. Add the salmon fillets and sear for 2 minutes on one side. Turn and sear for 1 minutes on the second side. Sprinkle with the pepper. Reduce the heat to low, then pour in the white wine and 2 tablespoons of the lemon juice. Cover and cook until the juices are nearly absorbed and the fish is halfway cooked, about 3 minutes. Uncover and pour in 2 more tablespoons of the lemon juice and 3 tablespoons of the water. Re-cover and cook just until the fish flakes easily with a fork, about 3 minutes longer. Most of the pan juices will have been absorbed.

Place a salmon fillet on each mound of greens. Raise the heat to high, add the remaining 4 tablespoons lemon juice and the remaining 1 tablespoon water, and deglaze the pan, stirring to dislodge any browned bits from the pan bottom. Pour the pan juices evenly over the fish and serve.

Serves 8

Shrimp, Avocado, and Tomato Salad

Cumin adds an unexpected but pleasing flavor to the lime vinaigrette. This salad is equally good served as a first course or as a light lunch. The dressing can be made up to 2 hours ahead. Cover and let stand at cool room temperature.

To make the vinaigrette, whisk together the lime juice, cumin, lime zest, garlic, mustard, salt, and pepper. Whisk in the olive oil. Set aside.

To make the salad, bring a saucepan three-fourths full of water to a boil. Add the shrimp and cook until they curl and turn pink, about 3 minutes. Drain and pat dry. Peel and devein and place in a large non-aluminum bowl. Add half of the vinaigrette to the shrimp, toss well, and let stand for 10 minutes.

Meanwhile, halve, pit, and peel the avocados and cut lengthwise into slices $^1/_2$ inch (12 mm) thick. Core and halve the tomatoes and cut into wedges $^1/_2$ inch (12 mm) wide. Add the avocados, tomatoes, and cilantro to the shrimp and toss gently.

Place the salad greens in a separate bowl. Whisk the remaining vinaigrette and pour over the greens. Toss well. Divide the greens among individual plates. Top with the shrimp mixture. Season each serving with several grinds of pepper and serve at once.

Serves 6

FOR THE VINAIGRETTE

2 tablespoons lime juice

2 teaspoons ground cumin

$1^1/_2$ teaspoons grated lime zest

1 teaspoon minced garlic

$^1/_2$ teaspoon Dijon Mustard

$^1/_2$ teaspoon salt

$^1/_4$ teaspoon ground pepper

5 tablespoons ($2^1/_2$ fl oz/75 ml) olive oil

FOR THE SALAD

24 large shrimp (prawns) in the shell, 1–$1^1/_4$ lb (500–625 g) total weight

2 ripe avocados

6 small yellow or red tomatoes or a combination of the two, about $^3/_4$ lb (375 g) total weight

3 tablespoons chopped fresh cilantro (fresh coriander)

6 cups (9 oz/280g) packed mixed salad greens

Ground pepper to taste

Salade Niçoise

FOR THE DRESSING

¼ cup (2 fl oz/60 ml) red wine vinegar

1½ tablespoons Dijon mustard

1 tin (2 oz/60 g) flat anchovy fillets in olive oil, drained and minced

2 garlic cloves, minced

⅔ cup (5 fl oz/160 ml) olive oil

Salt and ground pepper to taste

FOR THE SALAD

3 (6 oz/185 g) cans tuna, preferably packed in olive oil

Generous pinch of salt

1½ lb (750 g) small red boiling potatoes

6 eggs

1¼ lbs (625 g) green and yellow beans, trimmed

2 heads butter (Boston) lettuce, cleaned, trimmed, and separated into leaves

4 large tomatoes, each cut into 6 wedges

⅓ cup (1½ oz/50 g) tiny black olives, preferably Niçoise

To make the dressing, in a small bowl whisk together the vinegar, mustard, anchovies, and garlic. Slowly whisk in the olive oil. Season with salt and pepper. Set aside.

Drain the tuna and separate into chunks. Set aside.

Place the potatoes in a large pot, then carefully place the eggs on top of them. Add water to cover and place over medium-high heat, bring to a simmer, then adjust the heat to maintain a gentle simmer. Using a slotted spoon, remove the eggs after 8 minutes and rinse under cold water until cool. Add salt to the water and continue cooking the potatoes until easily pierced with the tip of a sharp knife, 10–12 minutes longer, then lift them out with a slotted spoon and set aside.

Add about 2 cups (16 fl oz/500 ml) of water to the pot along with some salt. Raise the heat to high and bring the water to a boil. Add the beans and cook until just tender, about 5 minutes. Drain, rinse with cold water, drain again, and pat dry.

Peel the hard-boiled eggs and halve or quarter them lengthwise. Peel the potatoes, if desired, and cut into slices.

Arrange the lettuce leaves on a platter or in a large shallow bowl. Arrange the tuna, potatoes, eggs, beans, and tomato wedges on top. Scatter the olives over the salad, drizzle with the dressing, and serve.

Serves 6

Chopped Chicken Salad

This versatile salad can accommodate the odds and ends of raw vegetables that tend to accumulate in the refrigerator bin. Instead of fennel, mushrooms, or radishes, try cucumber, zucchini (courgette), celery, or cauliflower.

Put the chicken breast halves in a large saucepan over medium heat. Add the 2 cups chicken broth, or more as needed to cover. Bring to a simmer, adjust the heat to keep the broth just below a simmer, and cook, uncovered, until the chicken is just white throughout, 10–15 minutes. Using a slotted spoon, transfer the chicken breasts to a cutting board; reserve the broth for another use. When the chicken is cool, cut into a small dice.

To make the dressing, in a bowl, whisk together the lemon juice, tarragon, mustard, and garlic. Gradually whisk in the olive oil. Season with salt and pepper. Set aside to allow the flavors to blend.

In a large bowl, combine the romaine, fennel, mushrooms, radishes, carrots, radicchio, and red onion.

Add the chicken to the dressing and stir to coat, then add the chicken and all the dressing to the vegetables. Toss well. Taste and adjust the seasonings. The salad may need more lemon, as it should taste quite lemony.

Serves 6

2 lbs (1 kg) skinless, boneless chicken breast halves

2 cups (16 fl oz/500 ml) chicken broth, or more as needed

FOR THE DRESSING

1/2 cup (4 fl oz/125 ml) lemon juice, or to taste

1/4 cup (1/3 oz/10 g) minced fresh tarragon

2 tablespoons Dijon mustard

3 cloves garlic, minced

1 cup (8 fl oz/250 ml) olive oil

Salt and ground pepper to taste

3 romaine lettuce hearts, trimmed and chopped

1 fennel bulb, trimmed and chopped

3/4 lb (12 oz/375 g) mushrooms, brushed clean and chopped

1 bunch radishes, chopped

3 carrots, peeled and chopped

1 head radicchio, chopped

1 medium red onion, chopped

Smoked Chicken and Fennel Salad with Almonds

If you can't find smoked chicken breasts, you can smoke regular bone-in breasts at home in a smoker or over low indirect heat on a regular charcoal grill, adding more coals as the chicken cooks. Remove the meat from the bones after smoking.

¼ cup (1¼ oz/37 g) slivered blanched almonds

2 fennel bulbs, about 1¼ lb (625 g) total weight

4 smoked boneless, skinless chicken breast halves, cut into strips about 1 inch (2.5 cm) long and ¼ inch (6 mm) wide

1 large shallot, minced

1 cup (8 fl oz/250 ml) mayonnaise

1 tablespoon finely grated lemon zest

½ teaspoon Dijon mustard

Salt and ground pepper to taste

About 18 red leaf or butter (Boston) lettuce leaves

Preheat an oven to 350°F (180°C). Spread the almonds on a baking sheet and toast until golden and fragrant, 5–7 minutes. Remove from the oven and let cool.

Meanwhile, cut off the stems, feathery tops, and any bruised outer stalks from the fennel bulbs. Chop the bulbs, then chop enough of the feathery tops to yield 1 tablespoon. Place the chopped fennel bulbs, chicken, shallot, and almonds in a bowl. Toss to mix.

In a large bowl, whisk together the mayonnaise, lemon zest, and mustard until smooth. Add the fennel-chicken mixture and mix well. Season with salt and pepper. Cover and refrigerate for 30 minutes.

Line 6 serving plates with the lettuce leaves. Spoon the fennel-chicken mixture on top. Sprinkle with the chopped fennel tops and serve.

Serves 6

Double-Bread and Chicken Salad

Fresh tomatoes are delectable when combined with garlicky croutons, crisp bits of chicken, and arugula. Although this main-course salad tastes best when the chicken is hot, it can also be served cold or warm. Basil can be used in place of the arugula.

To make the croutons, preheat an oven to 400°F (200°C). Spread the bread cubes on a baking sheet and drizzle evenly with the olive oil. Bake until lightly golden, about 15 minutes. Stir and continue to bake until golden brown, about 10 minutes longer. Let cool for a few minutes. Rub with the garlic. Set aside.

Meanwhile, make the dressing: In a large bowl, combine the olive oil, vinegar, garlic, salt, and pepper; mix well.

To make the salad, add the tomatoes to the bowl with the dressing and turn in the dressing until well coated. Set aside. Pour oil into a sauté pan to a depth of 1 inch (2.5 cm). Place over medium-high heat and heat until a bread cube dropped into the oil sizzles immediately upon contact. While the oil is heating, place the bread crumbs on a plate. Roll the chicken pieces, a few at a time, in the crumbs until coated. Transfer to a sheet of waxed paper. When you have coated enough pieces to fill the sauté pan in a single layer, spoon the chicken into the pan and fry until just cooked through, 3–4 minutes. Using a slotted spoon, transfer to paper towels to drain. Repeat until all the chicken is cooked.

Add the hot chicken to the bowl of tomatoes and dressing. Then add the arugula, reserving 1 tablespoon for garnish, and all but 5 or 6 of the croutons. Turn all the salad ingredients to coat the croutons and the chicken with the dressing.

To serve, scoop the salad into a serving bowl. Top with the reserved croutons and arugula.

Serves 4–6

FOR THE CROUTONS

2 cups (4 oz/125 g) cubed day-old baguette (1-inch/2.5-cm cubes)

2 tablespoons olive oil

2 cloves garlic

FOR THE DRESSING

1/3 cup (3 fl oz/80 ml) extra-virgin olive oil

3 tablespoons red wine vinegar

2 cloves garlic, crushed

1/2 teaspoon salt

1/2 teaspoon ground pepper

FOR THE SALAD

2 lb (1 kg) tomatoes, chopped

Canola, sunflower, or other light oil for frying

1 cup (4 oz/125 g) seasoned, fine dried bread crumbs

1 1/2 lb (750 g) boneless chicken breast, cut into 1-inch (2.5-cm) pieces

1 cup (2 oz/60 g) coarsely chopped arugula (rocket)

Bangkok Chicken Salad

This refreshing and spicy salad is even easier to make with leftover cooked chicken breasts and store-bought shredded carrots. Look for dried rice noodles, also known as *maifun* or rice vermicelli, in well-stocked grocers or Asian markets.

1 lb (500 g) skinless, boneless chicken breast halves

1/3 cup (1/2 oz/15 g) chopped fresh mint

1/4 cup (1 1/4 oz/37 g) peeled and minced fresh ginger

3 large cloves garlic, minced

1 large jalapeño chile, minced

1/4 cup (2 fl oz/60 ml) reduced-sodium soy sauce

3 tablespoons lime juice

3 tablespoons honey

2 teaspoons Asian sesame oil

1 head napa cabbage, 1 1/4 lb (625 g)

3 oz (90 g) dried rice stick noodles

2 cucumbers, peeled, halved, seeded, and sliced

2 cups (10 oz/310 g) shredded carrots

6 green (spring) onions, chopped

Preheat an oven to 375°F (190°C). Place the chicken in a single layer on a baking sheet. Cover with aluminum foil. Bake until cooked through, about 15 minutes. Remove from the oven, discard the foil, and let cool. Shred the meat; set aside.

In a bowl, stir together the mint, ginger, garlic, chile, soy sauce, lime juice, honey, and sesame oil. Set aside.

Remove 8 of the outer leaves from the cabbage head and reserve.

Cut out the core and then finely shred the remaining leaves; you should have about 4 cups (12 oz/375 g). Set aside.

Bring a large saucepan three-fourths full of water to a boil. Add the noodles and cook until tender, about 4 minutes. Drain and rinse under cold running water. Drain again and cut into 2-inch (5-cm) lengths.

In a large bowl, combine the shredded cabbage, chicken, cucumbers, carrots, green onions, noodles, and soy sauce mixture. Let stand for 20 minutes to allow the flavors to blend.

Line a serving bowl with the reserved cabbage leaves. Mound the salad in the center. Serve immediately.

Serves 8

Soups

Wonton Soup

To make the ginger juice for this soup, grate ginger to a fine paste, place in a small, fine-mesh sieve, and press with the back of a spoon to extract the juice. The wontons can be made in advance and refrigerated for up to 1 day or frozen for up to 1 month.

FOR THE WONTONS

¹/₂ lb (250 g) ground (minced) pork

¹/₄ lb (125 g) peeled shrimp (prawns), chopped

¹/₄ cup (1¹/₂ oz/45 g) finely minced water chestnuts

¹/₄ cup (1 oz/30 g) finely minced green (spring) onions

1 egg

2 tablespoons light soy sauce

1 tablespoon dry sherry

2 teaspoons Asian sesame oil

1 teaspoon ginger juice (see note)

Salt to taste, if needed

1 package (1 lb/500 g) wonton wrappers

2 teaspoons cornstarch (cornflour) dissolved in 2 tablespoons water

8 cups (64 fl oz/2 l) chicken broth simmered with 3 slices peeled fresh ginger for 10 minutes

1 bunch spinach, stems removed and leaves cut into strips

To make the wontons, in a medium bowl, combine the pork, shrimp, water chestnuts, and green onions. In a small bowl, whisk together the egg, soy sauce, sherry, sesame oil, and ginger juice. Stir the egg mixture into the pork mixture, mixing well. Bring a saucepan three-fourths full of water to a boil, add a small ball of the pork mixture to the water, and poach until cooked through, 2–3 minutes. Drain, taste, and adjust the seasonings with soy, ginger, or a little salt.

To assemble the wontons, lay out 10 wonton wrappers on a work surface. Place a teaspoon or so of the mixture on the center of each wrapper. Dip your finger in the cornstarch mixture and spread along two edges of each wrapper. Fold each in half on the diagonal to form a triangle and press the seams to seal securely. Place on a baking sheet. Repeat until all the stuffing is used; you should have about 48 wontons. Wrap any leftover wrappers airtight and store in the refrigerator for up to 1 week. Refrigerate the wontons until needed.

In a large saucepan, bring the stock to a boil over high heat, then reduce the heat to low to maintain a gentle simmer. At the same time, bring a large saucepan half full of water to a boil. Carefully drop the wontons into the boiling water. When the water returns to a boil, add 1¹/₂ cups (12 fl oz/375 ml) cold water. When the water returns to a boil, add 1 more cup (8 fl oz/250 ml) cold water. Return to a boil again, then reduce the heat to low and simmer until the filling is cooked through, about 5 minutes. Using a slotted spoon, transfer the wontons to the simmering broth. Add the spinach and simmer until it wilts, about 1 minute. To serve, ladle into 6 large warmed bowls, dividing the wontons evenly.

Serves 6

Minestrone

If using dried beans, pick over and discard any misshapen beans or stones. Rinse, drain, and place in a pot with water to cover by 2 inches (5 cm). Bring to a boil, boil for 2 minutes, then cover, remove from the heat, and let stand for 1 hour. Drain and return to the pot with fresh water to cover by 2 inches (5 cm). Bring to a boil, reduce the heat to low, cover, and simmer until tender, 45–60 minutes. Add salt during the last 10 minutes of cooking. If using canned beans, drain and rinse well.

In a large soup pot over medium heat, warm the olive oil. Add the onions and cook, stirring, until softened and translucent, about 10 minutes. Add the pancetta and cook, stirring, until tender, about 5 minutes longer. Add the carrots and celery and cook, stirring, until beginning to soften, just a few minutes. Add the tomatoes and enough water or broth to cover amply. Bring to a boil, reduce the heat to low, cover, and simmer until the tomatoes break down, about 10 minutes.

Meanwhile, if desired, place half of the white beans in a food processor or blender with a little of the cooking liquid or, if using canned beans, a little broth. Purée until smooth.

Add the potatoes, zucchini, green beans, white beans (including puréed, if using), Swiss chard (if using), and pasta and simmer until the vegetables and pasta are cooked, about 15 minutes. Stir often to prevent sticking. Swirl in the 2 tablespoons extra-virgin olive oil. Season with salt and pepper.

Remove from the heat and stir in the pesto. Ladle into warmed bowls and serve immediately. Pass the Parmesan at the table.

Serves 4

½ cup (3½ oz/105 g) dried small white beans or 1 can (15 oz/470 g) white beans

Salt to taste

2 tablespoons olive oil

2 yellow onions, diced

½ cup (3 oz/90 g) diced pancetta

3 carrots, peeled and sliced

2 celery stalks, diced

¾ lb (375 g) tomatoes, peeled, seeded, and diced

5–6 cups (40–48 fl oz/1.25–1.5 l) water or chicken broth, or as needed

4 small new potatoes, unpeeled, diced

2 zucchini (courgettes), halved lengthwise and sliced

¼ lb (125 g) green beans, trimmed and cut into 1-inch (2.5-cm) lengths

2 cups (4 oz/125 g) chopped Swiss chard (optional)

¼ lb (125 g) macaroni

2 tablespoons extra-virgin olive oil

Ground pepper to taste

¼ cup (2 oz/60 g) pesto (page 290)

¼ cup (1 oz/30 g) grated Parmesan cheese

Hot-and-Sour Broth with Mushrooms

This simple broth is a suitable first course for nearly any Asian-inspired meal. Look for chile paste with garlic in well-stocked food stores and Asian markets. If fresh oyster or cremini mushrooms are unavailable, substitute fresh white mushrooms.

1 oz (30 g) dried Chinese black mushrooms

½ cup (4 fl oz/125 ml) boiling water

1 lemongrass stalk, white part only, or grated zest of 1 lime

6 cups (48 fl oz/1.5 l) chicken broth

¼ cup (2 fl oz/60 ml) lime juice

1 tablespoon peeled and finely chopped fresh ginger

2 teaspoons fish sauce

½–1 teaspoon chile paste with garlic (see note)

1 cup (3 oz/90 g) thinly sliced fresh oyster or cremini mushrooms

1 clove garlic, minced

2 teaspoons soy sauce

Salt to taste

2 green (spring) onions, sliced on the diagonal

Place the dried mushrooms in a small bowl and add the boiling water. Let stand until softened, about 30 minutes. Drain, reserving the liquid. Remove the stems and discard. Slice the caps. Strain the liquid through a sieve lined with cheesecloth (muslin). Set aside the sliced mushrooms and soaking liquid.

If using the lemongrass, cut into 2-inch (5-cm) lengths and crush with the side of a knife.

In a saucepan, combine the lemongrass or lime zest, broth, lime juice, ginger, fish sauce, and chile paste with garlic. Add the sliced reconstituted mushrooms and their soaking liquid. Bring to a boil over high heat. Reduce the heat to medium and simmer, uncovered, until the broth is infused with the seasonings, about 20 minutes.

Using a slotted spoon, remove the lemongrass pieces and discard. Stir in the fresh mushrooms and garlic and cook until soft, about 5 minutes. Stir in the soy sauce and taste and adjust the seasonings with salt.

Ladle into warmed bowls and garnish with the green onions. Serve immediately.

Serves 4

Miso Soup with Tofu and Mushrooms

Miso is a nutritious protein-rich paste made from fermented ground soybeans mixed with rice, wheat, or barley. Red (*aka*) miso or white (*shiro*) miso can be used to make this soup; the former has a heartier flavor.

Using a damp kitchen towel, wipe, but do not wash, the kombu. In a saucepan over medium heat, combine the kombu and the water. Slowly bring almost to a boil, then remove the kombu. Return the water to a boil and add the bonito flakes; do not stir. Immediately remove from the heat and let the flakes sink to the bottom of the pan. Pour the stock through a very fine-mesh sieve set over a large bowl. Discard the flakes.

Return 1/2 cup (4 fl oz/125 ml) of the stock to the saucepan, add the miso and stir until thoroughly combined. Add the remaining stock and the mirin or sake. If using enoki mushrooms, cut off the lower portion of the stems and discard. If using shiitakes, cut off the stems and discard. Thinly slice the caps. Bring the stock almost to a boil over medium heat. Add the mushrooms and tofu. Remove from the heat.

Ladle the soup into warmed bowls, garnish with the green onion, and serve at once.

Serves 4–6

1 piece kombu seaweed, about 4 inches (10 cm) long

4 cups (32 fl oz/1 l) water

1 cup (1/2 oz/15 g) loosely packed dried bonito flakes

1/3 cup (3 1/2 oz/105 g) red or white miso

1 tablespoon mirin or sake

2 oz (60 g) fresh enoki mushrooms and/or fresh shiitake mushrooms

1/4 lb (125 g) soft tofu, cut into 1/2-inch (12-mm) cubes

1 green (spring) onion, including tender green tops, cut on the diagonal into thin slices

Matzo Ball Soup

If you would like to use homemade chicken stock (page 288) for this soup, begin with 12 cups (3 qts/3 l) and boil over high heat until reduced by half. (The matzo balls can be cooked several hours in advance and reheated in the soup just before serving.)

4 eggs

1/3 cup (3 fl oz/80 ml) tap water or seltzer water

3 tablespoons rendered chicken fat or melted and cooled margarine

1/2 teaspoon salt, plus salt to taste

1/4 teaspoon ground white pepper, plus white pepper to taste

1 1/4 cups (7 oz/220 g) matzo meal

6 cups (48 fl oz/1.5 l) chicken broth

2 cups (12 oz/375 g) diced cooked chicken (optional)

1 cup (5 oz/155 g) diced cooked carrots (optional)

1 cup (5 oz/155 g) shelled English peas (optional)

1/4 cup (1/3 oz/10 g) chopped fresh parsley

In a large bowl, whisk together lightly the eggs and tap or seltzer water. Add the chicken fat or margarine and stir until the fat is mixed in. Add the 1/2 teaspoon salt and the 1/4 teaspoon white pepper. Gradually pour in the matzo meal, adding it in a steady stream while stirring with a spoon. Do not overbeat. Cover and chill for 30 minutes.

Line 2 large baking sheets with parchment (baking) paper. Using a large soup spoon dipped in cold water and wet hands, form the chilled matzo mixture into balls about 1 1/2 inches (4 cm) in diameter. Do not roll too compactly. Place on the prepared baking sheets, cover, and refrigerate for at least 30 minutes or up to 3 hours or until ready to cook.

Bring 2 large saucepans three-fourths full of salted water to a boil over high heat. Drop in the matzo balls, cover the pans, and allow the water to return to a boil. Immediately reduce the heat to low and simmer until doubled in size and cooked through, 30–40 minutes. To test, cut into a ball; it should be cooked uniformly to the center. Using a slotted spoon, transfer to a plate and set aside.

Bring the broth to a boil in a large saucepan over high heat. Reduce the heat to low to maintain a gentle simmer and season with salt and pepper. Add the matzo balls and the chicken, carrots, and/or peas, if using. Simmer until all the ingredients are heated through, 8–10 minutes. To serve, ladle into warmed bowls, dividing the matzo balls evenly, and sprinkle with the parsley.

Serves 6

Chilled Cucumber Soup with Radish Confetti

This light and refreshing soup is a delicious start to a meal. For other colorful garnishes, try shredded carrots, or finely diced tomato. Chopped fresh dill may be substituted for the green (spring) onions.

Finely dice enough cucumber to measure $^1/_3$ cup (2 oz/60 g); set aside. Chop the remaining cucumber and place in a blender or food processor with the onion, buttermilk, and yogurt. Process until smooth. Season with salt and pepper. Cover and refrigerate until cold, about 30 minutes.

To serve, divide the soup among chilled bowls and garnish with the reserved cucumber, the radish, and the green onion. Serve at once.

Serves 4

2 lb (1 kg) cucumbers, peeled, halved, and seeded

$^1/_3$ cup (1$^1/_2$ oz/45 g) chopped yellow onion

1 cup (8 fl oz/250 ml) low-fat buttermilk

$^1/_2$ cup (4 oz/125 g) fat-free plain yogurt

Salt and ground pepper to taste

$^1/_3$ cup (1$^1/_2$ oz/45 g) diced radish

$^1/_4$ cup ($^3/_4$ oz/20 g) finely chopped green (spring) onion tops

Roasted Eggplant Soup

In the summer, garnish this soup with chopped tomatoes and basil or a dollop of pesto. In the fall, try roasted red pepper purée, and in the winter, chopped oil-packed sun-dried tomatoes mixed with thyme.

3 eggplants (aubergines)

3 tablespoons unsalted butter or olive oil

1 large yellow onion, chopped

2 cloves garlic, minced

1–2 tablespoons peeled and grated fresh ginger (optional)

5 cups (40 fl oz/1.25 l) chicken or vegetable broth, plus extra for thinning (optional)

1/2 cup (4 fl oz/125 ml) heavy (double) cream (optional)

Salt and ground pepper to taste

3/4 cup (6 fl oz/180 ml) heavy (double) cream

Grated zest and juice of 1 lemon

3 tablespoons chopped fresh flat-leaf (Italian) parsley

Preheat an oven to 450°F (230°C).

Using a fork, prick the eggplants in a few places and place on a baking sheet. Bake, turning once or twice to ensure even cooking, until very tender, about 1 hour. Remove from the oven and, when cool enough to handle, cut in half and scoop out the flesh from the skins into a colander, discarding any large pockets of seeds. Place the colander in the sink and let the eggplant pulp drain to rid it of bitter juices, 20–30 minutes. Coarsely chop the pulp and set aside.

In a saucepan over medium heat, melt the butter or warm the oil. Add the onion and sauté, stirring occasionally, until tender, about 10 minutes. Add the garlic and the ginger, if using, and sauté until fragrant, about 2 minutes. Add the eggplant pulp and 5 cups (40 fl oz/1.25 l) broth, raise the heat to high, and bring to a boil. Reduce the heat to low and simmer for a few minutes to meld the flavors. Remove from the heat and let cool slightly. Working in batches, purée the soup in a blender or food processor and return to a clean saucepan. Reheat gently, thinning to the desired consistency with additional broth or with the 1/2 cup (4 fl oz/125 ml) cream, if the eggplant is acidic or sharp in flavor. Season with salt and pepper.

In a bowl, beat the 3/4 cup (6 fl oz/180 ml) cream just until soft peaks form. Fold in the lemon zest and juice.

Ladle the soup into warmed individual bowls and garnish with a dollop of the whipped cream and a sprinkling of parsley. Serve hot.

Serves 6

Corn Chowder

Using both yellow and white kernels makes this summertime chowder particularly attractive. The Red Pepper Cream spices each portion without overwhelming the natural sweetness of the fresh corn.

Make the Red Pepper Cream, if desired. Set aside.

To make the chowder, place the salt pork or bacon in a heavy saucepan over medium-low heat. Cook, stirring occasionally, until the fat is rendered and the salt pork or bacon is crisp, about 5 minutes. Using a slotted spoon, transfer the crisp bits to a plate and reserve for another use. Raise the heat to medium-high, add the celery and onion to the fat in the pan, and sauté until nearly translucent, 5–6 minutes.

Raise the heat to high, pour in the chicken broth, and deglaze the pan, stirring to dislodge any browned bits from the pan bottom. Add the potatoes, thyme, bay leaf, salt, and pepper and return to a boil. Cover, reduce the heat to low, and cook until the potatoes are just tender, 10–15 minutes. Add the milk and simmer for 5 minutes. Add the corn and simmer just until the corn is tender, 3–4 minutes.

To serve, ladle the soup into warmed bowls. Place a spoonful of the Red Pepper Cream, if using, on top of each serving.

Serves 6–8

Red Pepper Cream (page 290), optional

FOR THE CHOWDER

1 tablespoon chopped salt pork or 2 slices bacon, chopped

1/4 cup (1 1/2 oz/45 g) finely diced celery

1 small yellow onion, finely diced

2 cups (16 fl oz/500 ml) chicken broth

4 or 5 red new potatoes, about 3/4 lb (375 g) total weight, diced

2 tablespoons fresh thyme leaves

1 bay leaf

1/2 teaspoon salt

1/2 teaspoon ground pepper

2 cups (16 fl oz/500 ml) milk, heated

Kernels from 6 ears of corn, preferably a mixture of white and yellow

Potato, Corn, and Avocado Chowder

Inspired by Colombian *ajiaco*, this filling soup has an appealing variety of textures.
It makes a delicious prelude to a simple meal of grilled sausages or, paired with
a salad of crisp greens, it can be a flavorful meal on its own.

2 tablespoons canola oil

1 yellow onion, chopped

6 green (spring) onions, chopped

2 cloves garlic, minced

2 russet potatoes, about 1 lb (500 g) total weight, peeled if desired, and cubed

1 garnet yam or sweet potato, about 1/2 lb (250 g), peeled and cubed

2 white or yellow potatoes, about 1 lb (500 g) total weight, peeled and cubed

8 cups (64 fl oz/2 l) chicken broth or water

1/2 cup (3/4 oz/20 g) chopped fresh cilantro (fresh coriander)

Salt and ground white or black pepper to taste

1 1/2 cups (9 oz/280 g) corn kernels (cut from about 3 ears)

1 cup (8 fl oz/250 ml) milk or light (single) cream

1 avocado, pitted, peeled, and chopped, tossed with 2 tablespoons lime juice

In a saucepan over medium-high heat, warm the oil. Add the yellow and green onions and sauté until softened, about 5 minutes. Stir in the garlic and the russet potatoes, yam or sweet potato, and white rose or Yellow Finn potatoes. Pour in the broth or water and add half of the cilantro. Bring to a boil, reduce the heat to low, and simmer, uncovered, until the potatoes are soft and the flavors are blended, about 20 minutes. Season with salt and pepper.

Add the corn and the milk or cream. Simmer until the corn is tender, about 5 minutes longer; do not allow to boil. If you like, mash some of the potatoes with a fork to thicken the soup.

To serve, stir in the remaining cilantro and ladle the chowder into warmed soup bowls. Top with the avocado, dividing evenly.

Serves 4–6

Fresh Corn Soup

Sometimes the early summer white corn is so sweet you think that sugar has been added. For this recipe, you may want to combine white corn for sweetness and yellow corn for body.

2 red bell peppers (capsicums) or 3 poblano chiles (optional)

Lemon juice to taste (optional)

¼ cup (2 oz/60 g) unsalted butter

1 yellow onion, diced

Kernels from 10 ears of corn, 8–10 cups (3–3¾ lb/1.5–1.75 kg)

6 cups (48 fl oz/1.5 l) water or chicken broth, or as needed

Salt and ground pepper to taste

Sugar to taste, if needed

Shredded Monterey jack cheese (optional)

Preheat a broiler (griller). If using bell peppers, cut in half lengthwise and remove the skin, seeds, and ribs. Place, cut sides down, on a baking sheet. Broil (grill) until the skins blacken and blister. If using chiles, broil (grill) them whole, turning as necessary to blacken evenly. Remove from the broiler, drape the peppers or chiles loosely with aluminum foil, let cool for 10 minutes, and then peel away the skins. If using the chiles, slit lengthwise and remove and discard the stems and seeds. Purée or chop them (you will need to chop if you plan on using jack cheese as well) and reserve for garnishing. If using bell peppers, purée in a blender or food processor and season with a little lemon juice, if desired. Reserve for garnishing the soup.

In a large saucepan over medium heat, melt the butter. Add the onion and sauté, stirring occasionally, until tender and translucent, about 10 minutes. Add the corn, stir well, and cook for 2 minutes to blend with the onion. Pour in the water or chicken broth; it should just barely cover the corn. Raise the heat to high and bring to a boil. Reduce the heat to medium and simmer, uncovered, until the corn is tender, about 6 minutes. Remove from the heat and let cool slightly.

Working in batches, purée the soup in the blender. Then pass the purée through a food mill fitted with the coarse disc or a coarse-mesh sieve placed over a clean saucepan. Place over medium-high heat and reheat to serving temperature. Season with salt, pepper, and with sugar, if needed. Add more broth if the soup is too thick.

To serve, ladle into warmed bowls and top each with a swirl of the pepper purée and a little jack cheese, if desired.

Serves 6

Corn and Roast Poblano Soup

The flavor of this soup is enhanced by roasting the poblano chiles before adding them and steeping the cumin seeds, bay leaves, rosemary, and chipotle chiles in warm milk to infuse the milk with their flavors.

Preheat a broiler (griller). Place the poblano chiles on a baking sheet. Broil (grill), turning as needed, until the skins blacken and blister. Remove from the broiler, drape the chiles loosely with aluminum foil, and let cool for 10–15 minutes. Working under cold running water, peel away the skins. Slit lengthwise and remove the stems, seeds, and ribs. Pat the chiles dry and then dice them. Set aside.

Pour the milk into a heavy saucepan. In a small, dry frying pan over high heat, toast the cumin seeds, shaking the pan constantly until they begin to change color, about 4 minutes. Remove from the heat and add to the milk. Add the chipotle chiles, bay leaves, and rosemary and place over low heat. Cover and bring to a gentle simmer; do not allow to boil. Remove from the heat and let stand, covered, for 20 minutes.

Meanwhile, in a stockpot over medium heat, melt the butter with the olive oil. Add the onions and salt and sauté, stirring, until the onions are soft and golden brown, 15–20 minutes. Reduce the heat to medium-low, add the garlic and ground cumin, and sauté, stirring constantly, until aromatic, about 5 minutes. Stir in the corn and poblano chiles, and continue cooking until the corn is lightly browned, about 5 minutes. Using a fine-mesh sieve, strain the milk into the corn mixture. Bring to a gentle simmer and continue to simmer until the flavors have melded, about 15 minutes. Remove from the heat and let cool for a few minutes.

In a food processor, purée one-third of the soup. Return the purée to the stockpot, stirring well. If necessary, place over low heat to reheat gently. Taste and adjust the seasonings. Ladle into soup bowls, garnish with the green onions, and serve.

Serves 6

6 or 7 large poblano chiles

8 cups (64 fl oz/2 l) milk

2 tablespoons cumin seeds

1 or 2 chipotle chiles

2 bay leaves

1 large fresh rosemary sprig or ½ teaspoon dried rosemary

2 tablespoons unsalted butter

2 tablespoons olive oil

2 large yellow onions, diced

2 teaspoons salt

4–6 cloves garlic, minced

2 teaspoons ground cumin

Kernels cut from 8 ears of corn (about 8 cups/3 lb/1.5 kg)

6 green (spring) onions, including about 2 inches (5 cm) of green, finely chopped

Roasted Tomato Soup with Tiny Meatballs

Preheat an oven to 400°F (200°C). Arrange the tomato and onion pieces, cut sides down, on a large baking sheet. Drizzle with the olive oil and lay the thyme and rosemary sprigs on top. Roast until the tomatoes begin to char and the onions are tender, about 45 minutes. Remove from the oven and let cool slightly.

Meanwhile, make the meatballs: In a bowl, combine the bread crumbs and ¹/₂ cup (4 fl oz/125 ml) of the water. Let soften, about 5 minutes. Add the meat, egg, cheese, sage, 1 teaspoon of the salt, and pepper. Mix well. Cover and chill for 1 hour.

While the meat is chilling, cook the rice: In a heavy saucepan over high heat, bring the remaining 1 cup (8 fl oz/250 ml) water to a boil. Add the rice, reduce the heat to low, cover, and cook until the rice is tender and all the water has been absorbed, about 15 minutes.

Pass the tomatoes, onion, and juices through a food mill placed over a large bowl. Discard the solids. (Alternatively, purée in a food processor, then pass the purée through a fine-mesh sieve into a large bowl.) Measure the tomato mixture; there should be about 6 cups (48 fl oz/1.5 l). Add enough meat or vegetable broth to measure 8 cups (64 fl oz/2 l) total. Transfer to a large saucepan and place over medium heat. Bring to a simmer, reduce the heat to very low, and cover.

Shape the meat mixture into tiny balls each about ³/₄ inch (2 cm) in diameter. There should be about 25 meatballs. Slip the meatballs into the broth, re-cover, raise the heat to low, and simmer gently until cooked through, about 5 minutes. Add the rice and heat through. Season with salt and pepper. While the rice is heating, finely chop together the parsley, orange zest, and garlic.

Ladle the soup into warmed bowls, distributing the meatballs evenly. Sprinkle with a little of the parsley mixture and serve immediately.

Serves 6–8

4 lb (2 kg) ripe tomatoes, halved crosswise

1 large sweet onion, such as Vidalia, cut into wedges

¹/₂ cup (4 fl oz/125 ml) extra-virgin olive oil

2 fresh thyme sprigs

1 fresh rosemary sprig

³/₄ cup (1¹/₂ oz/45 g) coarse fresh bread crumbs

1¹/₂ cups (12 fl oz/375 ml) water

¹/₂ lb (250 g) ground (minced) veal, turkey, or lean pork

1 egg

¹/₄ cup (1 oz/30 g) grated Parmesan cheese

1 tablespoon torn fresh sage leaves

1 teaspoon salt, plus salt to taste

Ground pepper to taste

¹/₂ cup (2 oz/60 g) Arborio rice

About 2 cups (16 fl oz/500 ml) beef or vegetable broth

¹/₃ cup (¹/₂ oz/15 g) firmly packed fresh flat-leaf (Italian) parsley leaves

1 orange zest strip, 3 inches (7.5 cm) long

1 clove garlic

Spicy Tomato Soup

Cayenne or hot-pepper sauce adds a subtle touch of fire to this soup, while a garnish of yogurt counteracts the heat. Fresh tomatoes will yield the best flavor. For tips on peeling them, consult the technique section (page 291).

2 tablespoons pure olive oil

1 yellow onion, finely chopped

1 carrot, peeled and grated

4 cloves garlic, chopped

1/4 teaspoon cayenne pepper or a dash of hot-pepper sauce such as Tabasco, plus cayenne pepper for garnish

3 lb (1.5 kg) tomatoes, peeled, seeded, and chopped

1 1/3 cups (11 fl oz/340 ml) chicken broth

Salt and ground black pepper to taste

1/2 cup (4 oz/125 g) plain yogurt

1/4 cup (1/3 oz/10 g) minced fresh dill, flat-leaf (Italian) parsley, or snipped fresh chives

In a saucepan over medium-high heat, warm the oil. Add the onion and carrot and sauté until softened, about 5 minutes. Add the garlic and 1/4 teaspoon cayenne pepper or hot-pepper sauce and sauté until the garlic has softened, about 30 seconds. Add the tomatoes and broth and bring to a boil. Reduce the heat to medium and simmer, uncovered, until the flavors are blended, at least 20 minutes or for up to 45 minutes. The longer the mixture cooks, the smoother it will become.

Working in batches, transfer the soup to a blender or food processor and purée until smooth. Alternatively, pass through a food mill placed over a bowl. Return to the saucepan, place over medium-high heat, and season with salt and pepper. Heat to serving temperature.

Ladle into warmed bowls and top each serving with a dollop of yogurt and a sprinkling of dill or other herb. Dust with cayenne pepper and serve immediately.

Serves 4–6

Avocado Soup with Shrimp and Salsa

Usually served chilled, this Latin American soup is also delicious at room temperature. The zesty tomato salsa provides a lively contrast to the rich and creamy flavor of the avocado. Fresh cooked crabmeat can be substituted for the shrimp, if you like.

Working in 2 or 3 batches, combine the avocados, broth, and cream in a blender. Purée until smooth. Adjust the amount of cream used as needed for a good soup consistency. Transfer to a bowl. Stir in the lemon juice and season to taste with salt, and pepper. Cover and refrigerate until cold but not overly chilled, about 1 hour.

Meanwhile, make the tomato salsa: In a bowl, combine the tomato, onion, chiles, garlic, lemon or lime juice, cilantro, olive oil, salt, and pepper. Stir well, taste, and adjust the seasonings.

To serve, remove the soup from the refrigerator, taste, and adjust the seasonings. Ladle the soup into chilled individual bowls. Top each serving with some of the diced shrimp and a generous dollop of the salsa.

Serves 6–8

3 large avocados, halved, pitted, peeled, and diced

3 cups (24 fl oz/750 ml) chicken broth, or as needed

1–1½ cups (8–12 fl oz/250–375 ml) heavy (double) cream

2 tablespoons lemon juice

Salt and ground pepper to taste

FOR THE TOMATO SALSA

1½ cups (10½ oz/330 g) finely chopped tomato

⅓ cup (2 oz/60 g) minced red onion

2 or 3 jalapeño chiles, minced

2 cloves garlic, minced

3 tablespoons lemon or lime juice, or to taste

¼ cup (⅓ oz/10 g) chopped fresh cilantro (fresh coriander)

¼ cup (2 fl oz/60 ml) olive oil

Salt and ground pepper to taste

12–16 cooked shrimp (prawns), peeled and diced

Mexican Vegetable Soup

Make this soup in summer when corn, tomatoes, and zucchini are at their best. If you like spice, leave the seeds in the chiles. Serve with corn tortillas toasted on both sides in a frying pan over medium-high heat or simply warmed in the oven.

2 tablespoons vegetable oil

3 small leeks, white and pale green parts only, halved and thinly sliced

3 small carrots, peeled and diced

1¹/₂ jalapeño chiles, seeded and minced

3 small cloves garlic, minced

1 cup (6 oz/185 g) peeled, seeded, and chopped tomatoes

6 cups (48 fl oz/1.5 l) chicken broth

3 cups (24 fl oz/750 ml) water

Salt to taste

3 bone-in chicken thighs

3 small zucchinis (courgettes), diced

3 tablespoons chopped fresh cilantro (fresh coriander)

2 cups (12 oz/370 g) corn kernels

Heat the vegetable oil in a saucepan over medium heat. Add the leeks, carrots, chiles, and garlic and sauté until the vegetables are softened, about 5 minutes. Add the tomato and sauté for 3 minutes longer. Add the broth and water. Bring to a simmer and season with salt. Add the chicken, cover partially, and simmer gently until the chicken is cooked through, about 20 minutes.

Using tongs, transfer the chicken to a cutting board and let cool. Add the zucchini and cilantro to the soup and simmer gently until the zucchini is just tender, 5–10 minutes. Stir in the corn and simmer until tender, about 2 minutes.

Remove and discard the skin from the chicken thighs, then remove the meat from the bones. Shred or coarsely chop the meat, stir into the soup, and heat through. Taste and adjust the seasonings.

Ladle into warmed bowls and serve hot.

Serves 6

Tomato and Garden Vegetable Soup

Preheat an oven to 425°F (220°C). Line 2 rimmed baking sheets with aluminum foil and brush with olive oil.

Using a sharp knife, cut the tomatoes crosswise in half. Working over a sieve placed over a large measuring pitcher, gently squeeze out the seeds from the tomatoes, capturing all the juices. Press the contents through the sieve. Add enough of the tomato juice to measure 3 cups (24 fl oz/750 ml) total. Set aside. Coarsely chop the tomato halves. Separate the garlic head into cloves, leaving the skins intact, and reserve 2 cloves. In batches, arrange the tomatoes, the remaining unpeeled garlic cloves, the zucchini, yellow squashes, carrots, potatoes, celery, corn, and 1 each of the chopped onions and leeks on the prepared baking sheets. Season each batch with a pinch of salt and a few drops of olive oil. Roast until lightly browned on the edges and nearly tender, 10–15 minutes. Remove from the oven. When the garlic has cooled slightly, gently squeeze the cloves free of their skins back into the vegetables, leaving the soft cloves whole.

Meanwhile, peel and mince the reserved 2 garlic cloves. In a large stockpot over medium heat, melt the butter with the 1 tablespoon olive oil. Add the minced garlic and the remaining chopped onion and leek, and sauté until soft, 5–6 minutes. Add all of the roasted vegetables, the tomato juice, and the chopped parsley, basil, and savory, and stir to mix well. Season with salt and pepper, and add the broth and parsley sprigs. Bring to a boil, reduce the heat to low, cover partially, and simmer until tender, about 15 minutes. Discard the parsley sprigs. Taste and adjust the seasonings.

To serve, ladle the soup into warmed bowls, top with the croutons, and sprinkle with the minced herbs and grated Parmesan. Serve at once.

Serves 10–12

6–8 large firm, ripe tomatoes

About 1½ cups (12 fl oz/375 ml) tomato juice, or as needed

1 small head garlic

2 *each* zucchini (courgettes) and yellow summer squashes, diced

4 *each* carrots and potatoes, peeled and diced

4 celery stalks, finely diced

Kernels cut from 4 ears of corn

2 *each* yellow onions and leeks, white part only, chopped

Salt and ground pepper to taste

Olive oil as needed, plus 1 tablespoon olive oil

2 teaspoons unsalted butter

2 tablespoons chopped fresh flat-leaf (Italian) parsley, plus minced parsley for garnish

1 tablespoon *each* chopped fresh basil and chopped fresh summer savory, plus minced basil and summer savory for garnish

8 cups (64 fl oz/2 l) chicken broth

7 or 8 parsley sprigs, tied together

Croutons (page 290) and grated Parmesan cheese for garnish

Gazpacho Verde

Here, tomatillos stand in for the ripe red tomatoes that are the usual base for this cold summer soup from Spain. Toasted walnuts take the place of the bread that thickens the soup. Green tomatoes make an interesting substitute for the tomatillos.

1 lb (500 g) tomatillos, husks removed

1 yellow onion, sliced

2 jalapeño chiles, halved and seeded

¼ cup (1 oz/30 g) walnuts

1 green bell pepper (capsicum), seeded and coarsely chopped

1 English (hothouse) cucumber, peeled and coarsely chopped

2 cloves garlic

2 tablespoons olive oil

Juice of 1 lime

1 tablespoon minced fresh flat-leaf (Italian) parsley

Salt and ground black pepper to taste

Cayenne pepper to taste

1 jicama, peeled and diced

Preheat an oven to 375°F (190°C). Lightly oil a baking sheet.

Place the tomatillos, onion slices, and jalapeños on the prepared baking sheet. Roast until the tomatillos and the onions are lightly browned and softened, and the jalapeños are blackened and blistered, 18–20 minutes. Remove from the oven and let cool.

Reduce the oven temperature to 350°F (180°C). Spread the walnuts on another, ungreased baking sheet and toast until fragrant and just beginning to brown, 5–7 minutes. Remove from the oven and let cool.

Place the cooled vegetables and nuts in a blender or food processor along with the bell pepper, cucumber, garlic, olive oil, lime juice, and parsley. Process until smooth. Transfer to a nonaluminum bowl and season with salt, black pepper, and cayenne pepper. Cover and chill for at least 2 hours or for up to 3 hours.

Ladle into chilled bowls and garnish each serving with a spoonful of diced jicama. Serve immediately.

Serves 6

Garden Gazpacho with Garlic Toasts

To make the soup, combine the cucumbers, tomatoes, bell pepper, lemon juice, and olive oil in a blender or food processor. Process until just blended. Do not purée; the mixture should be slightly chunky. Transfer to a nonaluminum bowl and stir in the garlic, cilantro, pepper, and salt. Cover and chill for at least 1 hour or for up to 12 hours.

Meanwhile, make the toasts: Preheat an oven to 400°F (200°C). Place the bread slices on a baking sheet and drizzle evenly with the olive oil. Toast in the oven until slightly golden on top, about 15 minutes. Turn and continue to toast until golden on the second side, 10–15 minutes longer. Remove from the oven. Rub both sides of each slice with the garlic cloves. Set aside to cool.

Just before serving, place the condiments in separate small bowls.

To serve, place 3 baguette slices in the bottom of each soup bowl. Stir the soup and ladle it over the bread in the bowls. Accompany with the condiments, to be added to the soup as desired.

Serves 4

FOR THE SOUP

1½ cucumbers, peeled, seeded, and coarsely chopped

3 large, firm, ripe tomatoes, peeled and coarsely chopped

1 red bell pepper (capsicum), seeded and coarsely chopped

2 teaspoons lemon juice

1 tablespoon olive oil

1 clove garlic, minced

1½ tablespoons coarsely chopped fresh cilantro (fresh coriander)

1 teaspoon ground pepper

½ teaspoon salt

FOR THE TOASTS

12 baguette slices

2 tablespoons olive oil

2 cloves garlic

FOR THE CONDIMENTS

½ cucumber, peeled, seeded, and chopped

1 tomato, peeled and chopped

2 or 3 green (spring) onions, chopped

2 serrano chiles, seeded, if desired, and thinly sliced

¼ cup (⅓ oz/10 g) chopped fresh cilantro (fresh coriander)

Yellow Pepper Soup

This soup is best during the summer months, when bell peppers are at their peak of flavor. Red peppers also make a beautiful soup. For a special-occasion dinner, make half the recipe with yellow peppers and half the recipe with red.

¼ cup (2 fl oz/60 ml) olive oil

1 yellow onion, diced

1 carrot, peeled and minced

1 celery stalk, diced

6 cups (48 fl oz/1.5 l) vegetable broth

8 large yellow bell peppers (capsicums), halved and seeded

1 teaspoon minced fresh thyme

Salt and ground pepper to taste

6–12 fresh flat-leaf (Italian) parsley leaves

In a large saucepan over medium heat, warm the olive oil. Add the onion, carrot, and celery and sauté, stirring constantly, until golden brown, 5–7 minutes.

Add the broth, raise the heat to high, and bring to a boil. Add the peppers, reduce the heat to medium, cover, and simmer until the peppers are very tender, 30–35 minutes. Remove from the heat.

Working in batches, and using a slotted spoon, transfer the peppers, onion, carrot, and celery to a blender or food processor. Add some of the cooking liquid and purée until smooth. Return to the saucepan and place over medium heat.

Add the thyme, bring to a simmer, and cook, uncovered, for 10 minutes to blend the flavors. Season with salt and pepper.

Ladle into warmed soup bowls or mugs and garnish each bowl with 1 or 2 parsley leaves. Serve at once.

Serves 6

Asparagus Soup

The addition of potato and only a little milk or cream offers a light richness to this satisfying soup. Look for asparagus with tightly closed tips. When the tips start to open, it is a sign that asparagus are no longer at their peak and are less sweet.

Cut 1 inch (2.5 cm) off the tips of the asparagus spears. Set aside.

Cut the remaining asparagus into 2-inch (5-cm) lengths. Bring a large saucepan three-fourths full of salted water to a boil. Add the asparagus tips and parboil for 2 minutes. Drain and immediately immerse the tips in cold water to halt the cooking. Drain, pat dry with paper towels, and set aside.

In a large saucepan over medium heat, melt the butter. Add all the asparagus except the tips and sauté, stirring occasionally, until well coated with the butter, 2–3 minutes. Add the potato and about 3 cups (24 fl oz/750 ml) of the broth or just enough to cover the asparagus. Cover the pan, bring to a boil, then reduce the heat to low, and simmer until the asparagus and the potato are very tender and just about falling apart, about 20 minutes. Remove from the heat.

Working in batches, purée the soup in a blender or food processor. Return the purée to a clean saucepan and add the remaining 1–2 cups (8–16 fl oz/250–500 ml) broth as needed to achieve the desired consistency. Then add the milk or cream if a little richness is desired. Reheat gently over low heat, adding the reserved asparagus tips. Season with salt and pepper.

Ladle the soup into warmed bowls and sprinkle with the parsley or mint. Serve hot.

Serves 6

2½ lb (1.25 kg) asparagus, tough ends removed

¼ cup (2 oz/60 g) unsalted butter

1½ cups (7½ oz/235 g) peeled and diced russet potato

4–5 cups (32–40 fl oz/1–1.25 l) vegetable or chicken broth

About ½ cup (4 fl oz/125 ml) milk or heavy (double) cream (optional)

Salt and ground pepper to taste

3 tablespoons chopped fresh flat-leaf (Italian) parsley or mint

Mushroom, Carrot, and Leek Soup

The broth in this light, flavorful soup is a combination of rich chicken and beef broths and carries a colorful array of finely cut vegetables. The soup can be made 1 day in advance, covered, and refrigerated. Reheat over medium heat.

2 tablespoons unsalted butter

2 tablespoons vegetable oil

4 carrots, peeled and cut into julienne strips

2 leeks, white part only, halved lengthwise and sliced crosswise 1/4 inch (6 mm) thick

1 lb (500 g) fresh shiitake mushrooms, brushed clean, stems discarded, and caps cut into julienne strips

1/4 lb white fresh mushrooms, brushed clean and thinly sliced

2 teaspoons finely chopped garlic

3 cups (24 fl oz/750 ml) beef broth

3 cups (24 fl oz/750 ml) chicken broth

1/2 teaspoon salt

1/4 teaspoon ground pepper

Wedge of good-quality Parmesan cheese

4 fresh flat-leaf (Italian) parsley sprigs

In a large, deep-sided saucepan over medium-high heat, melt the butter with the vegetable oil. When hot, add the carrots and cook, stirring, until slightly softened, 2–3 minutes. Add the leeks and cook, stirring, until slightly softened, 3–4 minutes longer. Add the shiitake and white mushrooms and the garlic and cook, stirring, until softened and beginning to wilt, about 5 minutes.

Add the beef and chicken broths, salt, and pepper, and simmer, uncovered, until all the vegetables are tender, about 15 minutes. Taste and adjust the seasonings.

To serve, ladle into warmed individual bowls. Using a vegetable peeler or cheese slicer, shave thin slices from the wedge of Parmesan. Generously garnish each serving with the cheese and a parsley sprig.

Serves 4

Purée of Snow Pea and Leek Soup

For the best flavor, be sure to select young, tender snow peas for this elegant soup. It can also be refrigerated and served chilled; if you do, taste and adjust the seasoning before serving.

Place a heavy saucepan over medium heat. Coat the pan with nonstick cooking spray. Add the leeks, sprinkle with the sugar, and sauté, stirring frequently, until softened, about 8 minutes. Do not allow the leeks to color. Add the snow peas and sauté until they turn bright green, about 4 minutes. Remove 8 snow peas and set aside.

Add the broth to the pan and bring to a simmer. Simmer, uncovered, over medium heat until the peas are quite tender, about 8 minutes longer. Remove from the heat.

Purée the soup in a blender until smooth. Pour through a sieve placed over a clean saucepan, pressing hard on the solids with the back of a spoon. Discard the solids. Stir the milk into the purée and reheat gently. Season generously with salt and white pepper.

Meanwhile, in a small bowl, stir together the fromage blanc and tarragon. Season with white pepper. Cut the reserved snow peas into thin strips.

Ladle the soup into warmed bowls. Place a dollop of the fromage blanc on top of each serving and garnish with the julliened snow peas. Serve hot.

Serves 4

2 leeks, including 2 inches (5 cm) of green, chopped

2 teaspoons sugar

3/4 lb (375 g) snow peas (mangetouts), trimmed

3 cups (24 fl oz/750 ml) chicken broth

1/2 cup (4 fl oz/125 ml) low-fat milk

Salt and ground white pepper

1/4 cup (2 oz/60 g) fromage blanc

1 teaspoon chopped fresh tarragon

Creamy Mushroom Soup

Although fresh wild mushrooms such as chanterelles or porcini make for a particularly earthy and interesting soup, you can also make a delicious soup using cultivated white mushrooms, cremini, portobellos, or a combination.

1 oz (30 g) dried porcini

1 cup (8 fl oz/250 ml) hot water

6 tablespoons (3 oz/90 g) unsalted butter

2 yellow onions, chopped

2 lb (1 kg) fresh mushrooms (see note), brushed clean and thinly sliced

5 cups (40 fl oz/1.25 l) chicken broth

¼ cup (2 fl oz/60 ml) dry sherry or Madeira wine

1 cup (8 fl oz/250 ml) heavy (double) cream

Salt and ground pepper to taste

Ground nutmeg to taste

3 tablespoons chopped fresh flat-leaf (Italian) parsley

Rinse the dried porcini and place in a bowl. Add the hot water and let stand for about 1 hour. Lift out the porcini, squeezing them over the bowl to remove as much moisture as possible, and chop finely. Strain the soaking liquid through a sieve lined with damp cheesecloth (muslin) into a pitcher or bowl and set aside.

In a heavy saucepan over low heat, melt 2 tablespoons of the butter. Add the onions and sauté, stirring occasionally, until translucent and tender, about 10 minutes. Remove from the heat but leave in the pan.

In a large, wide sauté pan over medium heat, melt the remaining 4 tablespoons (2 oz/60 g) butter. Add the fresh mushrooms and cook slowly, stirring occasionally, until they give off their juices and soften, 10–15 minutes. If you like a coarser-textured soup, set aside some of the mushrooms to use as a garnish; keep warm.

Add the mushrooms in the sauté pan, the chopped porcini, and the strained mushroom liquid to the sautéed onions and return the pan to medium-high heat. Pour in the broth and bring to a boil. Reduce the heat to low and simmer, uncovered, until the broth is infused with the flavors, about 20 minutes.

Working in batches and using a slotted spoon, transfer the mushrooms and onions to a blender. Add a little of the cooking liquid and purée until smooth. Transfer to a clean saucepan. Thin the purée with as much of the remaining liquid as needed. Add the sherry or Madeira and cream and season with salt, pepper, and nutmeg. Reheat gently over low heat. Ladle into warmed bowls. If you have set aside mushrooms for garnish, divide them among the bowls, then sprinkle with the parsley.

Serves 6

Potato and Leek Soup with Dill

This creamy winter soup departs from the classic French recipe in the last-minute addition of fragrant fresh dill. On another occasion, substitute fresh tarragon for the dill. Serve with plenty of crusty French bread on the side.

In a large saucepan over medium-low heat, melt the butter. Add the leeks, stir to coat with the butter, cover, and cook, stirring occasionally, until the leek is soft, about 10 minutes. Add the potatoes and season with salt and pepper. Add the broth and water. Raise the heat to medium-high and bring to a simmer. Cover, adjust the heat to maintain a gentle simmer, and cook until the potatoes are completely tender, about 30 minutes. Remove from the heat and let cool slightly.

In a food processor or blender, purée the soup until completely smooth. Return to the saucepan and stir in the cream and dill. Reheat gently. Taste and adjust the seasonings.

Ladle into warmed mugs or bowls and serve hot.

Serves 6

6 tablespoons unsalted butter

6 small leeks, white and pale green parts only, halved and thinly sliced

6 small baking potatoes, peeled, halved lengthwise, and thinly sliced

Salt and ground pepper to taste

6 cups (48 fl oz/1.5 l) chicken broth

3 cups (24 fl oz/750 ml) water

1½ cups (12 fl oz/375 ml) heavy (double) cream

3 tablespoons minced fresh dill

Cold Lithuanian Beet Borscht

6–8 large beets, 3$^{1}/_{2}$–4 lb
(1.75–2 kg) total weight

About $^{1}/_{2}$ cup (4 fl oz/125 ml)
red wine

2 tablespoons unsalted butter

2 red (Spanish) onions, diced

1–1$^{1}/_{2}$ cups (8–12 fl oz/250–375
ml) chicken broth

3–4 cups (24–32 fl oz/
750 ml–1 l) buttermilk

Salt and ground pepper to
taste

2 tablespoons raspberry or
other fruit-flavored vinegar or
lemon juice, or to taste

Pinch of sugar (optional)

6 small or medium boiling
potatoes, peeled and coarsely
diced

1$^{1}/_{2}$ cups (7$^{1}/_{2}$ oz/235 g)
peeled, seeded, and diced
cucumber

$^{1}/_{2}$ cup (1$^{1}/_{2}$ oz/45 g) minced
green (spring) onion

3 hard-boiled eggs, peeled
and coarsely chopped

6 tablespoons (3 fl oz/90 ml)
sour cream or plain yogurt
(optional)

Peel 1 beet and grate it into a bowl. Pour in the red wine; it should cover the beet. Set aside. Trim the stems from the remaining beets, leaving about $^{1}/_{2}$ inch (12 mm) intact; do not peel. Place in a large saucepan, add water to cover, and bring to a boil. Reduce the heat to low, cover, and simmer until tender when pierced, 45–50 minutes. Drain, immerse in cold water to cool slightly, peel, then cut off the stems and root ends. Finely dice 1 cooked beet; set aside. Set the remaining beets aside separately.

In a small saucepan over medium heat, melt the butter. Add the onions and sauté until tender and translucent, about 10 minutes. Add broth to cover, raise the heat to high, and bring to a boil. Reduce the heat to low and simmer, uncovered, until the onions are very soft, about 10 minutes. Remove from the heat.

Slice the whole cooked beets and place in a blender. Add the cooked onions and their liquids and the grated beet and red wine and purée until smooth. Transfer to a bowl and add the buttermilk, using as much of it as is needed to balance the sweet and tart flavors of the soup. Season with salt and pepper. Add the vinegar or lemon juice and the sugar, if using. The balance of sweet and sour depends upon the taste of the cook, so add slowly and taste and adjust as you like. Stir in the reserved diced beet, cover, and refrigerate until well chilled, about 6 hours.

About 15 minutes before serving, place the potatoes in a saucepan with lightly salted water to cover. Bring to a boil, reduce the heat to medium, and simmer, uncovered, until just tender, 5–7 minutes. Drain well and keep hot.

To serve, ladle the soup into bowls. Garnish with the cucumber, green onion, hard-boiled eggs, and the hot potatoes. If desired, top each serving with a dollop of sour cream or yogurt or pass the bowl at the table.

Serves 6

Yellow Split Pea Soup

A pinch of toasted cumin seeds gives this soup a seductive fragrance. Enjoy any leftovers for lunch the next day; if desired, add a few tablespoons of minced ham when reheating.

3 tablespoons vegetable oil

3/4 teaspoon cumin seeds

3 large shallots, minced

3 clove garlic, minced

1 1/2 cups (8 oz/250 g) yellow split peas

6 cups (48 fl oz/1.5 l) chicken broth

3 small carrots, peeled and diced

6 oz (185 g) green beans, trimmed and cut into 1/2-inch (12-mm) lengths

3 cups (24 fl oz/750 ml) water

3 tablespoons chopped fresh cilantro (fresh coriander)

Salt and ground pepper to taste

In a soup pot over medium-high heat, warm the vegetable oil. When the oil is hot, add the cumin seeds. When the cumin seeds become fragrant and begin to darken, after about 1 minute, add the shallot and garlic. Cook, stirring, until the shallot is softened and beginning to color, about 2 minutes, reducing the heat if necessary to prevent burning.

Stir in the split peas and broth and bring to a simmer. Cover, adjust the heat to maintain a gentle simmer, and cook until the split peas are soft, about 45 minutes. Add the carrots, green beans, and water. Cover and simmer gently, stirring occasionally, until the split peas have dissolved into a near purée, about 30 minutes longer.

Stir in the cilantro, cover, and simmer for 5 minutes to blend the flavors. Season with salt and pepper. Ladle into a warmed bowls and serve hot.

Serves 6

Hearty Split Pea Soup

For an elegant presentation, add a few tablespoons of champagne to each bowl, garnish with a dollop of whipped cream flavored with lemon juice and grated lemon zest, and top with the crumbled bacon or pancetta.

Pick over the split peas and discard any misshapen peas or stones. Rinse the split peas and drain.

In a saucepan over medium heat, melt the butter. Add the onion and sauté, stirring occasionally, until tender and translucent, about 10 minutes. Add the split peas, carrots, bay leaf, and 6 cups (48 fl oz/1.5 l) water or broth. Raise the heat to high and bring to a boil. Cover, reduce the heat to low, and simmer until the peas are very soft, 45 minutes. If the mixture seems too thick, add more water or broth as needed. Discard the bay leaf. Add the spinach and simmer until it wilts, about 3 minutes.

Meanwhile, if using the bacon or pancetta, place a frying pan over medium heat. Add the bacon or pancetta slices and fry, turning as needed, until crisp, about 7 minutes. Transfer to paper towels to drain. When cool, crumble.

Remove the soup from the heat and let cool slightly. Working in batches, purée in a blender or food processor. Return to a clean saucepan and add milk, water, or broth as needed to thin to desired consistency. Place over medium-high heat and reheat to serving temperature. Season with the salt and pepper.

To serve, ladle into warmed bowls and sprinkle with the crumbled bacon or pancetta, if using.

Serves 4–6

2 cups (14 oz/440 g) dried split peas

2 tablespoons unsalted butter

1 large yellow onion, chopped

2 carrots, peeled and chopped

1 bay leaf

6 cups (48 fl oz/1.5 l) water or chicken broth, or as needed

1/2 lb (250 g) spinach, tough stems removed and finely chopped

3 slices bacon or pancetta (optional)

Milk for thinning (optional)

1 teaspoon salt

1/2 teaspoon ground pepper

Fresh Pea Soup with Chive Blossom Cream

English peas come into season at the same time chives are putting forth their delicate onion-flavored blossoms, and market vendors often sell chives with their blossoms intact. If unavailable, substitute a few blades of regular chives for each blossom.

In a small saucepan over medium-high heat, combine 3 of the chive blossoms and the cream. Bring to a boil, reduce the heat to low, and simmer, uncovered, until the cream thickens and is reduced by nearly half, 4–5 minutes. Remove from the heat and let stand for 30 minutes to allow the flavors to develop.

Separate the petals from the remaining 3 blossoms. Mince the petals and set them aside.

In a saucepan over medium-high heat, combine the chicken broth, peas, salt, and pepper. Bring to a boil, reduce the heat to low, and simmer until the peas are soft, 10–20 minutes. The timing will depend upon the size and maturity of the peas.

Remove from the heat and let cool slightly. Transfer to a blender or food processor and purée until smooth. Return the purée to the saucepan, place over medium heat, and heat to serving temperature.

Meanwhile, remove the whole chive blossoms from the cream and discard. Reheat the cream over medium heat until it is quite hot.

To serve, ladle the soup into warmed individual bowls. Add a spoonful of the cream to each serving and garnish with the minced petals. Serve immediately.

Serves 4

6 fresh chive blossoms

1 cup (8 fl oz/250 ml) heavy (double) cream

3 cups (24 fl oz/750 ml) low-sodium chicken broth

2 lb (1 kg) English peas, shelled

1 teaspoon salt

$\frac{1}{2}$ teaspoon ground white pepper

Bread and Onion Soup

Good-quality coarse country bread is essential for making this soup. Ideally, the bread should be a day old, as a drier loaf will absorb more liquid. If you must use fresh bread, toast it first to crisp it and concentrate its flavor.

¼ cup (2 oz/60 g) unsalted butter

6 large yellow onions, thinly sliced

6 tablespoons (³/₄ oz/20 g) chopped fresh basil

5 cups (40 fl oz/1.25 l) water, vegetable broth, or chicken broth

Salt and ground pepper to taste

4 thick (1-inch/2.5-cm) slices coarse country bread, preferably day-old, cut into 1-inch (2.5-cm) cubes

½ cup (2 oz/60 g) grated Parmesan or shredded fontina cheese

In a large sauté pan over low heat, melt the butter. Add the onions and sauté very slowly, stirring often, until caramelized, about 45 minutes. The onions must be sweet and golden but not brown. Stir in 2 tablespoons of the basil and cook for 5 minutes to flavor the onions. Add the water or broth, cover, and simmer until the onions are quite tender, about 30 minutes longer.

Meanwhile, preheat an oven to 350°F (180°C).

When the onion mixture is ready, season with salt and pepper and remove from the heat. Place individual ovenproof bowls on 1 or 2 baking sheets and evenly divide the bread cubes among them. Top with the hot onion mixture and then the cheese.

Bake until the cheese melts and the soup is piping hot, 10–20 minutes. Garnish with the remaining basil and serve.

Serves 6

Indian Red Lentil Soup

The Indian spices lighten and brighten the flavor of this simple soup. Red lentils have a tendency to break down into a coarse purée as they cook, so if you prefer some texture, omit the blender or food processor step.

1¹/₂ cups (10¹/₂ oz/530 g) red lentils

3 tablespoons unsalted butter

1 large yellow onion, chopped

2 tablespoons ground coriander

2 teaspoons ground cumin

2 teaspoons peeled and grated fresh ginger

¹/₂ teaspoon ground turmeric

Pinch of cayenne pepper

6 cups (48 fl oz/1.5 l) water, or vegetable, or chicken broth

1¹/₂ cups (9 oz/280 g) peeled, seeded, and diced tomatoes (fresh or canned)

2 tablespoons lemon juice, or to taste

Salt and ground black pepper to taste

3 tablespoons chopped fresh mint or cilantro (fresh coriander)

Pick over the red lentils and discard any misshapen lentils or stones. Rinse the lentils and drain.

In a saucepan over medium heat, melt the butter. Add the onion and sauté, stirring occasionally, until tender and translucent, 8–10 minutes. Add the coriander, cumin, ginger, turmeric, and cayenne and stir to mix well. Reduce the heat to low and cook, stirring occasionally, to release the flavors of the spices, 2–3 minutes. Add the lentils and then gradually add the water or broth, stirring constantly. Bring to a boil over high heat, reduce the heat to low, cover partially, and simmer until the lentils are very soft, 30–45 minutes.

Remove from the heat and let cool slightly. Working in batches, purée the soup in a blender or food processor. Return the soup to a clean saucepan and place over medium heat. Stir in the tomatoes and lemon juice and cook until heated through. Season with salt and black pepper.

To serve, ladle into warmed bowls and sprinkle with the mint or cilantro.

Serves 6

Oven-Dried Tomato and Lentil Soup

You can use 12 dry-packed sun-dried tomatoes in place of the oven-dried tomatoes. Soak them in 1¹/₂ cups (12 fl oz/375 ml) warm broth or warm water for 20 minutes. Drain and proceed as directed.

Preheat an oven to 250°F (120°C). Place the tomatoes, cut sides up, on a rack set on a baking sheet. Sprinkle with sea salt and place in the oven for about 2 hours. The tomatoes will dehydrate and intensify in flavor, but should still be a little soft. Remove from the oven and set aside.

Meanwhile, pick over the lentils and discard any damaged lentils or impurities. Rinse the lentils. Place in a bowl and add water to cover generously. Let soak for 1 hour. Drain and set aside.

In a saucepan over medium heat, warm the olive oil. Add the onion, carrot, and celery and sauté until golden brown, 5–7 minutes. Add the broth, drained lentils, and potatoes and bring to a boil. Reduce the heat to low and simmer, uncovered, until the lentils and potatoes are tender, 30–40 minutes.

Add the reserved tomatoes and the rosemary and continue to simmer, stirring gently to retain the shape of the tomatoes, until the flavors have blended, about 15 minutes longer. Season with salt and pepper.

Ladle into warmed bowls and serve hot.

Serves 6

6 plum (Roma) tomatoes, quartered lengthwise

Coarse sea salt

1¹/₂ cups (10¹/₂ oz/330 g) dried green lentils

3 tablespoons extra-virgin olive oil

1 yellow onion, minced

1 carrot, peeled and minced

1 celery stalk, minced

6 cups (48 fl oz/1.5 l) vegetable broth

1 lb (500 g) red new potatoes, unpeeled, quartered lengthwise

1 tablespoon minced fresh rosemary

Salt and ground pepper to taste

Caldo Verde

The dark green cabbage traditionally used in this Portuguese "green" soup is not widely available beyond Portugal's borders, but kale or collard greens make a good substitute. Thick slices of crusty corn bread make a delicious accompaniment.

Bring a saucepan three-fourths full of water to a boil. Prick the sausages with a fork and add to the boiling water. Boil for about 5 minutes. Using tongs, transfer the sausages to a cutting board and, when cool enough to handle, slice them. (You may discard the sausage-flavored water or reserve it for making the soup.)

Rinse and drain the greens, then remove any tough stems. Working in batches, stack the leaves, roll up the stack like a cigar, and cut crosswise into very, very thin strips. Set aside.

In a large saucepan over medium heat, warm the olive oil. Add the onions and sauté, stirring occasionally, until tender, about 10 minutes. Raise the heat to medium-high, add the potatoes and garlic, and sauté, stirring often, until slightly softened, about 5 minutes. Add the water or broth and 2 teaspoons salt, cover, and simmer over low heat until the potatoes are very soft, about 20 minutes.

Scoop out about 2 cups (10 oz/315 g) of the potatoes and mash well with a potato masher or fork. Return them to the pan, add the sliced sausage, and simmer until the sausage is cooked through, about 5 minutes longer. Add the greens, stir well, and simmer uncovered, stirring occasionally, for 3–5 minutes. Do not overcook; the greens should be bright green and slightly crunchy. Season with salt and pepper.

To serve, ladle into warmed bowls and drizzle each bowl evenly with extra-virgin olive oil.

Serves 6

½ lb (250 g) chorizo, linguiça, or kielbasa sausages

¾ lb (375 g) kale or collard greens

¼ cup (2 fl oz/60 ml) olive oil

2 large yellow onions, chopped

3 or 4 potatoes, 1–1¼ lb (500–625 g) total weight, peeled and thinly sliced

3 or 4 cloves garlic, finely minced

6–7 cups (48–56 fl oz/1.5–1.75 l) water or chicken broth

2 teaspoons salt, plus salt to taste

Ground pepper to taste

Extra-virgin olive oil for serving

Black Bean Soup

3 cups (21 oz/655 g) dried black beans

8 cups (64 fl oz/2 l) water

1 ham bone or ham hock

2 tablespoons olive oil

2 yellow onions, chopped

4 cloves garlic, minced

1 tablespoon ground cumin

1/2 teaspoon ground cinnamon

1/4 teaspoon ground cloves

1–2 tablespoons sherry vinegar

Salt and ground pepper to taste

FOR THE AVOCADO SALSA

1 large or 2 medium avocados, halved, pitted, peeled, and diced

1/2 cup (3 oz/90 g) seeded and diced tomato

1/4 cup (11/4 oz/37 g) finely diced red (Spanish) onion

Chopped fresh cilantro (fresh coriander) (optional)

1 small clove garlic, minced

1/2 small jalapeño chile, minced

2 tablespoons lime or lemon juice, or to taste

Salt to taste

Pick over the beans and discard any misshapen beans or stones. Rinse the beans, drain, and place in a saucepan. Add water to cover and bring to a boil over high heat. Boil for 2 minutes, then remove from the heat, cover, and let stand for 1 hour.

Drain the beans and return to the saucepan. Add the 8 cups (64 fl oz/2 l) water and the ham bone or ham hock. Bring to a boil over high heat. Cover partially, reduce the heat to low, and simmer.

Once the beans are simmering, in a large sauté pan over medium heat, warm the olive oil. Add the onions and sauté, stirring occasionally, until tender and translucent, about 10 minutes. Add the garlic, cumin, cinnamon, and cloves and cook for about 2 minutes longer. Add the onion mixture to the beans and simmer until very tender, 1–1 1/2 hours; the timing will depend upon the age of the beans.

Remove the soup from the heat. Remove the ham bone or ham hock and discard. Working in batches, purée the soup in a blender (or pass through a food mill). Return the soup to a clean saucepan and season with sherry vinegar and salt and pepper. Gradually reheat over medium heat, stirring often to prevent scorching. Thin with water if the soup is too thick, then taste and adjust the seasonings; it will probably need a little more salt.

Just before serving the soup, make the salsa: In a bowl, combine the avocados, tomato, onion, cilantro (if using), garlic, chile, lime or lemon juice, and salt. Toss well.

Ladle the soup into warmed individual bowls. Top each serving with a spoonful of the salsa, and serve at once.

Serves 8

Anasazi Bean Chili in Corn Cups

Pick over the beans and discard any damaged beans or impurities. Rinse the beans. Place in a bowl and add water to cover generously. Let soak for 3 hours. Drain.

Peel the tomatoes (see technique, page 291) and purée in a blender or food processor. In a stockpot over medium heat, warm the olive oil. Add the celery, carrots, and onions and sauté until softened, 6–8 minutes. Add the garlic, jalapeño chile, orange zest, broth, and drained beans. Bring to a boil, reduce the heat to low, and simmer gently, uncovered, stirring occasionally, until the beans are tender, about 2 hours.

About 30 minutes before the chili is ready, preheat an oven to 325°F (165°C). Lightly oil six 1-cup (8–fl oz/250-ml) ramekins or other individual baking dishes.

To make the corn cups, in a bowl, beat together the cream cheese and butter until creamy. Beat in the egg. In another bowl, stir together the all-purpose flour, masa harina, baking powder, and salt. Fold into the egg mixture, folding just until blended. Do not overmix.

Using your fingers, line the prepared ramekins or individual baking dishes with the mixture, dividing it evenly. Bake until a light golden brown, 18–20 minutes. Remove from the oven and keep warm.

When the chili is ready, add the chili powder, cumin, and coriander and season with salt and pepper. To serve, place a corn cup on each individual plate. Spoon the chili into the cups and garnish with the cilantro. Serve at once.

Serves 6

1³/₄ cups (12 oz/375 g) dried Anasazi or black beans

12 large tomatoes

5 tablespoons olive oil

5 celery stalks, diced

3 carrots, peeled and diced

2 large yellow onions, chopped

5 cloves garlic, minced

1 jalapeño chile, minced

2¹/₄ teaspoons grated orange zest

3 qt (3 l) vegetable broth

FOR THE CORN CUPS

¹/₂ cup (4 oz/125 g) *each* cream cheese and unsalted butter, at room temperature

1 egg

1¹/₃ cups (7 oz/220 g) all-purpose (plain) flour

²/₃ cup (3¹/₂ oz/105 g) masa harina

¹/₂ teaspoon baking powder

¹/₄ teaspoon salt

1 tablespoon chili powder

1 teaspoon *each* ground cumin and ground coriander

Salt and ground pepper to taste

¹/₄ cup (¹/₃ oz/10 g) minced fresh cilantro (fresh coriander)

Ribollita

Ribollita is Italian for "reboiled." First you make a hearty Tuscan vegetable soup, which is refrigerated overnight. The next day, you reheat ("reboil") the soup with slices of bread in it, which break down and thicken it further.

1½ cups (10½ oz/330 g) dried white beans, preferably cannellini

4 cups (32 fl oz/1 l) water

1 yellow onion

2 cloves garlic

1 bay leaf

2 teaspoons salt

½ cup (4 fl oz/125 ml) extra-virgin olive oil, plus more for drizzling

2 yellow onions, chopped

4 celery stalks, chopped

3 carrots, peeled and chopped

2 cloves garlic, minced

1 cup (6 oz/185 g) chopped canned plum (Roma) tomatoes

1–2 tablespoons tomato paste

1 lb (500 g) Savoy cabbage, tough stems removed and leaves coarsely chopped

1 tablespoon chopped fresh thyme

Salt and ground pepper to taste

6–8 slices coarse country bread

Pick over the beans, discarding any misshapen beans and stones. Rinse well and place in a saucepan with the water. Bring to a boil over high heat, boil for 2 minutes, then cover and remove from the heat. Let stand for 1 hour. Drain and return to the saucepan with fresh water to cover by about 2 inches (5 cm). Add the onion, garlic, and bay leaf and bring to a boil over high heat. Reduce the heat to low and simmer, uncovered, until the beans are tender but not falling apart, about 1 hour. Add the salt during the last 10 minutes of cooking. Remove and discard the onion, garlic, and bay leaf. Set the beans aside in their liquid.

In a large saucepan over medium heat, warm the ½ cup (4 fl oz/125 ml) olive oil. Add the onions, celery, carrots, and garlic and sauté, stirring, until the onions are tender, about 10 minutes. Add the chopped tomatoes and tomato paste and cook, stirring occasionally, for 5 minutes. Add the cabbage, the cooked white beans and their liquid, the thyme, the salt and pepper, and enough water just to cover the vegetables. Raise the heat to medium-high and bring to a boil. Cover, reduce the heat to low, and simmer until all the vegetables are very tender, about 2 hours. Remove from the heat, let cool, cover, and refrigerate for 8 hours or for up to 3 days.

Remove the soup from the refrigerator. Layer 2 or 3 bread slices in the bottom of a large saucepan. Ladle in enough soup just to cover. Repeat the layers until all the bread and soup are in the pan, ending with the soup. Slowly bring the soup to a boil over low heat, stirring often to make sure that the bottom doesn't scorch and to break up the bread, 20–30 minutes. It should eventually dissolve and form a thick soup. Scoop into warmed bowls and drizzle with the olive oil. Serve at once.

Serves 6

Stuffed-Cabbage Soup

Bring a large pot two-thirds full of salted water to a boil and drop in 1 cabbage. Simmer until the leaves loosen and are pliable, about 10 minutes. Transfer the cabbage to a colander and, when cool enough to handle, pull off the nicest large leaves. Repeat with the remaining cabbage head. You'll need about 18 leaves, or a few more if you want leftovers. Set the leaves aside. Reserve the remaining centers of the cabbage for another use.

To make the filling, in a blender or food processor, combine the eggs, onion, and garlic and purée. Transfer to a bowl and add the ground beef and rice. Mix well. Add the plumped raisins, pine nuts, and parsley and again mix well. Season with the allspice or cinnamon, and salt and pepper.

Place a heaping tablespoon or two of the filling on the lower third of each cabbage leaf. Fold in the sides, then roll up from the lower end and skewer closed with a toothpick. Repeat until all the filling is used.

In a deep, wide saucepan over medium heat, combine the broth, onion, and tomatoes. Bring to a simmer and carefully drop in the cabbage rolls. When the stock begins to boil very gently again, cover and simmer until very tender and fragrant, about 1 1/2 hours. Taste and adjust the seasonings.

To serve, using a slotted spoon, remove the cabbage rolls and place 3 rolls in each individual warmed bowl, discarding the toothpicks as you do. Ladle the hot broth over the rolls. Garnish with the parsley and dill and serve at once.

Serves 6

2 medium-large heads green cabbage, 1 1/2–2 lb (750 g–1 kg) each, cored

FOR THE FILLING

2 eggs

1 yellow onion, chopped

2 cloves garlic, minced

1 1/2 lb (750 g) ground (minced) beef

2 cups (14 oz/440 g) long-grain white rice

1/2 cup (3 oz/90 g) raisins, plumped in hot water and drained

1/4 cup (1 1/4 oz/37 g) pine nuts

1/4 cup (1/3 oz/10 g) chopped fresh parsley

1/4 teaspoon ground allspice or 1/2 teaspoon ground cinnamon

Salt and ground pepper to taste

7 cups (56 fl oz/1.75 l) beef or chicken broth, or as needed

1 yellow onion, chopped

1 cup (6 oz/185 g) peeled, seeded, and chopped tomatoes (fresh or canned)

3 tablespoons chopped fresh flat-leaf (Italian) parsley

3 tablespoons chopped fresh dill

Red Cabbage and Apple Soup

This hearty and delicious soup gets an extra burst of flavor from the grated apple added just before serving. Golden Delicious apples are sweet and finely textured, but if you want a sharper-flavored, crisper variety, choose Granny Smith instead.

1 head red cabbage, about ¾ lb (375 g)

4 Golden Delicious apples, about 1 lb (500 g) total weight

2 tablespoons unsalted butter

1 yellow onion, minced

¼ cup (2 fl oz/60 ml) red wine vinegar

4½ cups (36 fl oz/1.1 l) low-sodium beef broth

½ teaspoon salt

½ teaspoon ground pepper

2 teaspoons lemon juice

⅓ cup (3 fl oz/80 ml) light sour cream

¼ cup (⅓ oz/10 g) chopped fresh dill

On a cutting board, using a large, sharp knife, cut the cabbage in half through the stem end. Cut out the tough core portions and discard. One at a time, place each half, cut side down, on the board and cut into very thin slices. Cut 2 of the unpeeled apples into quarters, core them, and then cut into 1-inch (2.5-cm) cubes. Set the cabbage and the cut-up apples aside separately.

In a large saucepan over medium heat, melt the butter. When it is foaming, add the onion and sauté until translucent, 2–3 minutes. Add the apple cubes and sauté until softened slightly, another 3–4 minutes. Add the cabbage and sauté, stirring often, until it glistens and the color has lightened, 5–6 minutes. Add the vinegar and deglaze the pan, stirring to dislodge any browned bits from the pan bottom. Add the beef broth, salt, and pepper and bring to a boil over medium-high heat. Reduce the heat to low, cover, and simmer until tender, about 15 minutes.

While the soup is simmering, peel, halve, and core the remaining 2 apples, then shred them finely. Place the shredded apple in a small bowl, add the lemon juice, and toss to coat. Set aside.

When the soup is ready, remove from the heat and stir in three-fourths of the shredded apples. Ladle the soup into warmed bowls. Top each serving with a spoonful of the sour cream. Sprinkle the remaining grated apples and the dill over the top, dividing evenly. Serve at once.

Serves 4

Chickpea Stew

Wonderfully seasoned but not too spicy, this cold-weather stew is rich in protein. To save time, substitute 1 can (15 oz/470 g) chickpeas, drained and well rinsed, for the dried ones. Decrease the stock to 3 cups (24 fl oz/750 ml).

Pick over the chickpeas and discard any damaged beans or impurities. Rinse the chickpeas. Place in a bowl and add water to cover generously. Let soak for 3 hours. Drain.

In a saucepan over high heat, bring the broth to a boil. Add the chickpeas, reduce the heat to medium, and simmer, uncovered, until almost tender, about 1 1/2 hours. Add the potatoes, tomatoes, garam masala, ginger, and turmeric and continue to cook until the chickpeas and potatoes are tender, about 30 minutes longer.

Remove from the heat and let cool slightly. Transfer half of the broth and vegetables to a blender or food processor and purée until smooth. Return to the saucepan and season with salt and pepper. Reheat to serving temperature.

Ladle into warmed bowls, sprinkle with the cilantro, and serve hot.

Serves 6

3/4 cup (5 oz/155 g) dried chickpeas (garbanzo beans)

5 cups (40 fl oz/1.25 l) vegetable broth

1 lb (500 g) baking potatoes, peeled and diced

1 lb (500 g) tomatoes, peeled and chopped (see technique, page 291)

2 teaspoons garam masala (see glossary, page 293)

1/2 teaspoon ground ginger

1/2 teaspoon ground turmeric

Salt and ground pepper to taste

3 tablespoons chopped fresh cilantro (fresh coriander)

Butternut Squash Soup

1 butternut squash, 3$\frac{1}{2}$–4 lb (1.75–2 kg), halved, seeds and fibers discarded, peeled, and flesh cubed

4 leeks

1 large yellow onion, chopped

Coarse salt and ground black pepper to taste

2 tablespoons olive oil

3 carrots

5–6 cups (40–48 fl oz/1.25–1.5 l) chicken broth

1 teaspoon unsalted butter

1 celery stalk with leaves, chopped

1 teaspoon minced fresh thyme

Pinch of cayenne pepper

Pinch of freshly grated nutmeg, plus extra to taste

Preheat an oven to 425°F (220°C). Line 2 or 3 rimmed baking sheets with aluminum foil and brush with oil. Arrange the squash in a single layer on the prepared pans. Roast until browned on the edges, 13–15 minutes. Meanwhile, chop 2 of the leeks, including about 1 inch (2.5 cm) of the green. Remove the squash from the oven and set aside. Using the same pans, arrange the chopped leeks and onion in a single layer, and roast until browned on the edges, 10–12 minutes.

Meanwhile, julienne the remaining 2 leeks, using the white parts only. Using the same pans, scatter the julienned leeks in a single layer, season with salt and pepper, and drizzle with 1 tablespoon of the olive oil. Roast until crisp and browned, 12–13 minutes. Transfer to a paper towel–lined plate and set aside.

Peel and julienne 2 of the carrots. In a small frying pan over low heat, combine 2 tablespoons of the chicken broth and the julienned carrots. Cover partially and "sweat" the carrots until barely tender and the broth has evaporated, about 5 minutes. Transfer to the plate with the leeks.

Meanwhile, peel and chop the remaining carrot. In a stockpot over medium heat, melt the butter with the remaining 1 tablespoon oil. Add the celery and chopped carrot and sauté until the vegetables begin to soften, 5–6 minutes. Add the roasted chopped leeks, squash, and onion; cook for 1–2 minutes. Add the thyme, cayenne, nutmeg, and season with salt and pepper. Continue to cook, stirring, until the vegetables glisten, about 2 minutes. Add enough of the remaining chicken broth to cover the vegetables by $\frac{1}{2}$ inch (12 mm). Cover and bring to a boil. Reduce the heat to low, position the lid ajar, and simmer until all the vegetables are soft, about 20 minutes. Let cool for a few minutes, then purée the soup in a food processor.

Return the soup to the pot and reheat gently. Ladle into warmed soup bowls. Garnish with the reserved carrots and leeks, and a sprinkling of nutmeg.

Serves 6

Moroccan-Spiced Vegetarian Chili

Serve this richly spiced vegetarian chili with toasted pita points or on a bed of steamed couscous or rice. Other winter squashes such as Hubbard or acorn may be used in place of the butternut squash.

4 large ancho chiles

3 cups (24 fl oz/750 ml) water

4 large whole cloves garlic, plus 6 large cloves, sliced

1 yellow onion, chopped

1½ teaspoons *each* ground turmeric, cinnamon, cumin, and coriander

1 can (28 oz/875 g) chopped tomatoes

1 butternut squash, 1¼ lb (625 g), halved, seeded, peeled, and cut into ½-inch (12-mm) cubes

2 cans (15½ oz/485 g each) chickpeas (garbanzo beans)

2 zucchini (courgettes), cut into ½-inch (12-mm) dice

⅓ cup (2 oz/60 g) sliced dried apricots

⅓ cup (2 oz/60 g) sliced pitted prunes

In a saucepan, combine the chiles and water and bring to a boil. Remove from the heat. Cover and let stand for 15 minutes. Using tongs or a slotted spoon, transfer the chiles to a work surface; reserve the liquid. Discard the stems and seeds from the chiles. In a blender or food processor, combine the chiles with the 4 cloves garlic and ½ cup (4 fl oz/125 ml) of the liquid. Process until smooth. Set aside.

Heat a heavy pot over medium heat. Coat the pan with nonstick cooking spray. Add the onion, the sliced garlic cloves, turmeric, cinnamon, cumin, and coriander and sauté until the onion and garlic have softened, about 5 minutes. Stir in the tomatoes and their juices, butternut squash, and the chile purée. Cover and simmer, stirring occasionally, until the squash is just tender, about 25 minutes.

Stir in the chickpeas with their liquid, the zucchini, and dried apricots and prunes. Simmer, uncovered, until all of the squashes are tender, about 15 minutes longer. Transfer to a warmed serving dish and serve hot.

Serves 6

Spanish Pumpkin and Bean Soup

This chunky soup is made even more interesting with the addition of diced pears and a classic Catalan *picada* thickener of garlic, almonds, and bread. It is hearty enough to make a meal on its own.

Pick over the chickpeas and white beans, discarding any misshapen beans or stones. Rinse the chickpeas and beans and drain. Place in a bowl, add plenty of water to cover, and let soak overnight. The next day, drain them. In a saucepan over high heat, bring the 2 quarts (2 l) plus 3 cups (24 fl oz/750 ml) water to a boil. When the water is boiling, add the chickpeas and beans. When the water returns to a boil, reduce the heat to low and simmer until tender, about 1 hour.

Meanwhile, in a sauté pan over medium heat, warm 2 tablespoons of the olive oil. Add the onion and sauté, stirring occasionally, until tender, about 10 minutes. Stir in the ham and paprika, and then mix in the tomatoes. Cook for 10 minutes to blend the flavors. Add the saffron and liquid to the pan, mix well, and set aside.

Pour the remaining 6 tablespoons (3 fl oz/90 ml) olive oil into another sauté pan and place over medium heat. Add the almonds, bread, and garlic, and cook, stirring occasionally, until golden, about 5 minutes. Using a slotted spoon, transfer the almonds, bread, and garlic to a mortar or a small food processor. Grind with a pestle or process to a paste. Add the vinegar to the paste, mixing well. Set aside.

After the beans have cooked for 1 hour, add the pumpkin or butternut squash and the pears and simmer for 10 minutes. Finally, stir in the tomato-onion mixture, the green beans, and the bread mixture and simmer until the green beans and squash are tender and the flavors are blended, 10–15 minutes. Season with salt and pepper. Ladle into warmed bowls and serve immediately.

Serves 6–8

1 cup (7 oz/220 g) *each* dried chickpeas (garbanzo beans) and small dried white beans

2 qt (2 l) plus 3 cups (24 fl oz/750 ml) water

1/2 cup (4 fl oz/125 ml) olive oil

1 large yellow onion, chopped

1/4 cup (11/2 oz/45 g) diced ham

1 tablespoon sweet paprika

2 tomatoes, peeled, seeded, and diced

Pinch of saffron, steeped in 1/4 cup (2 fl oz/60 ml) hot water

12 almonds

1 slice bread, cut in half

2 cloves garlic

2 tablespoons sherry vinegar

11/2 cups (8 oz/250 g) peeled and coarsely chopped pumpkin or butternut squash

3 pears, halved, cored, peeled, and cut into chunks

1/2 lb (250 g) green beans, cut into 2-inch (5-cm) lengths

Salt and ground pepper to taste

Butternut Squash and Chipotle Soup

A sweet, mild purée of butternut squash provides the perfect backdrop for the intriguing smoky, spicy flavor of chipotle chiles. For this soup, you can use either canned chipotles or the ones sold loose.

Preheat an oven to 350°F (180°C). Cut the squash in half lengthwise. Using a spoon, scrape out the seeds and any fibers and discard. Place the squash halves, cut sides down, on a baking sheet and bake until just tender, about 35 minutes. Remove from the oven. When cool enough to handle, scoop out the flesh into a bowl.

In a large saucepan over medium-high heat, warm the corn oil. Add the bread and dried sage and sauté, stirring often, until the bread cubes are browned on all sides, about 4 minutes. Using a slotted spoon, transfer the croutons to a plate and set aside. Add the onion to the pan and sauté until softened, about 5 minutes. Stir in the squash, chiles, and broth. Bring to a simmer over medium heat and cook, uncovered, until the squash is very soft, about 30 minutes.

If using dried chiles, remove them from the pan, cut away their stems, then return the chiles to the soup. Working in batches, purée the soup in a blender until smooth. Taste and add salt as needed.

If the soup has cooled, return it to the pan and reheat gently. Ladle into warmed bowls. Divide the croutons among the servings and garnish with the sage leaves, if desired. Serve hot.

Serves 6

1 butternut squash, 2½ lb (1.25 kg)

1 tablespoon corn oil

2 slices coarse country bread, each about ½ inch (12 mm) thick, cut into ½-inch (12-mm) cubes

1 teaspoon dried sage

½ yellow onion, chopped

2 small chipotle chiles (see note)

3½ cups (28 fl oz/875 ml) chicken broth

Salt to taste

Fresh sage leaves (optional)

Sour Seafood Soup

2 tablespoons vegetable oil

1/2 lb (250 g) large shrimp (prawns), peeled and deveined, shells reserved

4 stalks lemongrass

8 green serrano chiles, halved

6 slices fresh galangal or 3 pieces dried galangal

6 cups (48 fl oz/1.5 l) chicken broth

8 fresh, frozen, or dried kaffir lime leaves

1 cup (4 oz/125 g) drained, canned straw mushrooms

1 cup (4 oz/125 g) drained, canned baby corn

1 tablespoon Thai roasted chile paste

1/2 lb (250 g) mussels, scrubbed and debearded

1/2 lb (250 g) bay scallops

1/4 lb (125 g) cleaned squid, cut crosswise into rings

3 tablespoons Thai fish sauce

2 tablespoons lime juice, or more to taste

1 red serrano chile, sliced crosswise, for garnish

2 tablespoons coarsely chopped fresh cilantro (fresh coriander), for garnish

In a saucepan over medium-high heat, warm the oil. Add the shrimp shells and sauté until bright orange, about 1 minute. Using a meat pounder, crush the lemongrass stalks slightly, cut into 2-inch (5-cm) pieces, and add to the shrimp shells. Add the green serrano chiles, galangal, chicken broth, and lime leaves and bring to a boil. Reduce the heat to low and simmer, uncovered, for 15 minutes.

Strain the stock through a colander placed over a stockpot; discard the shells and seasoning ingredients. Add the mushrooms, corn, and chile paste and stir to combine. Bring to a boil over high heat, uncovered. Add the shrimp and mussels, discarding any mussels that do not close to the touch. Cook, uncovered, until the shrimp turn bright orange and the mussels begin to open, about 3 minutes. Stir in the scallops and squid, and cook, uncovered, until the scallops and squid begin to feel firm, about 1 minute longer. Stir in the fish sauce and lime juice. Taste and adjust the seasonings. Discard any mussels that did not open.

Ladle the soup into warmed bowls, garnish with the red serrano chile and cilantro, and serve at once.

Serves 6

Asian Shrimp and Noodle Soup

Bring a large saucepan three-fourths full of salted water to a boil. Add the noodles, stir well, and parboil for 1–2 minutes. Drain and toss with a bit of vegetable oil. Set aside.

Cut up 5 of the green (spring) onions and place in a food processor. Add the shallots, garlic, lemongrass, jalapeño chile (include some of the seeds), and ginger. Pulse until a paste forms.

In a saucepan over medium heat, warm the 2 tablespoons vegetable oil. Add the paste and cook, stirring often, until fragrant, about 5 minutes. Add the broth and the lime zest and simmer for 5 minutes to infuse the broth with the flavors. Meanwhile, thinly slice the mushrooms and cut the snow peas lengthwise into 1/2-inch (12-mm) strips. Add to the broth along with the parboiled noodles, shrimp, and bean sprouts, and simmer until the shrimp turn pink, about 4 minutes. Season with the lime juice, salt, and pepper.

Finely mince the remaining 2 green (spring) onions and add to the soup along with the basil and mint. Immediately ladle into warmed soup bowls. Serve hot.

Serves 6

1/2–1 lb (250–500 g) fresh Chinese egg noodles

Vegetable oil for tossing noodles, plus 2 tablespoons

7 green (spring) onions

2 shallots

2 cloves garlic

1 lemongrass stalk, tender base portion only, cut into small pieces

1 jalapeño chile, cut up

2 tablespoons peeled and thinly sliced fresh ginger

9 cups (72 fl oz/2.25 l) low-sodium chicken broth simmered with 3 slices peeled fresh ginger for 10–15 minutes

1 tablespoon grated lime zest

1/4 lb (125 g) fresh white mushrooms, brushed clean

1/4 lb (125 g) snow peas (mangetouts)

1 lb (500 g) shrimp (prawns), peeled, deveined, and halved lengthwise

2 cups (4 oz/125 g) bean sprouts

2 tablespoons lime juice

Salt and ground pepper to taste

2 tablespoons *each* finely shredded fresh basil and mint

Seafood Stew with Tomatoes, Shrimp, and Scallops

1/4 cup (2 fl oz/60 ml) olive oil

2 yellow onions, chopped

2 small carrots, peeled and cut into 1/2-inch (6-mm) dice

2 teaspoons chopped garlic

2 cans (28 oz/875 g each) plum (Roma) tomatoes, drained and cut into 1/2-inch (12-mm) dice

3 cups (24 fl oz/750 ml) chicken broth

2/3 cup (5 fl oz/160 ml) dry white wine

2 tablespoons chopped fresh basil

2 teaspoons grated orange zest

1/2 teaspoon red pepper flakes

1/2 teaspoon salt

1 lb (500 g) Chilean sea bass, halibut, or other firm-fleshed whitefish fillet, skinned and cut into 1 1/2-inch (4-cm) cubes

3/4 lb (375 g) sea scallops

3/4 lb (375 g) large shrimp (prawns), peeled and deveined

2 tablespoons julienned fresh basil leaves

6 orange wedges, each cut 1/2 inch (12 mm) thick

In a large, heavy saucepan over medium heat, warm the olive oil. When hot, add the onions and carrots and sauté, stiring occasionally, until slightly softened, about 4 minutes. Add the garlic and cook for 1 minute, until fragrant. Add the tomatoes, broth, wine, basil, orange zest, red pepper flakes, and salt. Bring to a simmer, reduce the heat to low, and cook, uncovered, for about 10 minutes to blend the flavors.

Add the fish cubes and simmer for about 3 minutes. Add the scallops and shrimp and continue to simmer until the fish and scallops are opaque throughout and the shrimp are curled and pink, 2–3 minutes longer. Taste and adjust the seasonings.

Ladle into warmed shallow bowls. Sprinkle each serving with about 1 teaspoon julienned basil leaves and place an orange wedge alongside. Each diner should squeeze the juice from the orange wedge into the stew before eating.

Serves 6

Shrimp and Corn Chowder

To save time, have your fishmonger peel and devein the shrimp, just be sure to save the shells for use in the recipe. When simmered gently in water, the shells make a light-flavored broth that becomes a fragrant base for the soup.

Peel the shrimp, then cut each shrimp in half lengthwise, discarding the dark veinlike intestinal tract that runs along its back. Put the shells in a small saucepan with the water. Bring to a simmer over medium heat, adjust the heat to maintain a gentle simmer, and cook for 10 minutes. Strain, discarding the shells. Set the liquid aside.

In a saucepan over medium-low heat, fry the bacon until crisp, about 5 minutes. Using a slotted spoon, transfer to paper towels to drain. Add the butter and the green onion to the saucepan and sauté until the onion is softened, about 1 minute. Stir in the flour and cook, stirring, until smooth and slightly thickened, about 1 minute. Add the potatoes and the strained shrimp broth and bring to a simmer, stirring constantly. Cover and simmer gently until the potatoes are tender, about 10 minutes.

Add the corn, milk, parsley, the reserved shrimp, salt, and pepper to the saucepan and stir well. Bring just to a simmer, then stir in the bacon.

Ladle into warmed bowls and serve at once.

Serves 6

3/4 lb (375 g) large shrimp (prawns) in the shell

4 1/2 cups (36 fl oz/1.1 l) water

3 slices bacon, diced

2 tablespoons unsalted butter

1/3 cup (1 oz/30 g) minced green (spring) onion, white and pale green parts only

2 tablespoons all-purpose (plain) flour

3/4 lb (375 g) boiling potatoes, peeled and diced

2 cups (12 oz/370 g) corn kernels

3 cups (24 fl oz/750 ml) milk

1 tablespoon minced fresh parsley

Salt and ground pepper to taste

Roasted Asparagus and Shrimp Chowder

Toasting the asparagus and shrimp gives an intense flavor to this chunky soup. Reserve the feathery tops from the fennel bulb to use as a garnish. Deceptively light and healthy, it makes a lovely first course or a satisfying meal on its own.

10 large asparagus spears, tough ends removed

20 large shrimp (prawns), about 1 lb (500 g) total weight, peeled and deveined

2 teaspoons olive oil

1 small fennel bulb

1 leek, including 2 inches (5 cm) of green, chopped

1 small red bell pepper (capsicum), seeded and chopped

1 teaspoon herbes de Provence

3 cups (24 fl oz/750 ml) vegetable broth

1 russet potato, unpeeled, cut into 1/2-inch (12-mm) dice

1 cup (8 fl oz/250 ml) fat-free evaporated skimmed milk

Salt and ground pepper to taste

Preheat an oven to 425°F (220°C).

Place the asparagus and the shrimp on a baking sheet and drizzle with the olive oil. Toss to coat them with the oil and then spread out in a single layer.

Roast until the shrimp turn pink and opaque, about 5 minutes. Transfer to a plate. Turn the asparagus over and continue to roast until just tender, about 8 minutes longer. Remove from the oven and, when cool enough to handle, cut into 1-inch (2.5-cm) lengths.

Meanwhile, cut off the stems, feathery tops, and any bruised outer stalks from the fennel bulb. Reserve the tops for the garnish. Cut away and discard the core, then chop the bulb; set aside.

Heat a large saucepan over medium heat. Coat the pan with nonstick cooking spray. Add the fennel, leek, red pepper, and herbes de Provence and sauté until the vegetables are just beginning to soften, about 4 minutes. Add the broth and potato and bring to a simmer. Cook, uncovered, until the fennel is tender, about 15 minutes.

Pour in the milk and bring the soup back to a simmer. Add the shrimp and asparagus and stir until heated through. Season with salt and pepper. Ladle into warmed bowls. Garnish each serving with the reserved fennel tops. Serve hot.

Serves 6

Cioppino

In a large saucepan over medium heat, warm the olive oil. Add the onion and sauté, stirring occasionally, until translucent, about 5 minutes. Add the celery, garlic, bay leaves, thyme, fennel seeds, and red pepper flakes and cook until the celery is soft, about 5 minutes longer. Add the fish stock, tomatoes, wine, and tomato purée and simmer for about 10 minutes to blend the flavors. Season with salt and pepper.

Add the clams to the pan along with the lobster or crab. Cover and simmer briskly until the clams start to open, about 5 minutes. Add the mussels, shrimp, and scallops and continue to cook until the mussels open, the shrimp turn pink, and the scallops are opaque throughout, 3–5 minutes.

Ladle into warmed bowls and sprinkle with the parsley or basil. Serve immediately.

Serves 6

½ cup (4 fl oz/125 ml) olive oil

1 large yellow onion, chopped

3 stalks celery, chopped

3 tablespoons minced garlic

2 small bay leaves

2 fresh thyme sprigs

2 teaspoons ground fennel seeds

1 teaspoon red pepper flakes

5 cups (40 fl oz/1.25 l) fish stock

3 cups (18 oz/560 g) chopped canned plum (Roma) tomatoes, with their juices

1½ cups (12 fl oz/375 ml) dry red wine

½ cup (4 fl oz/125 ml) thick tomato purée

Salt and ground black pepper to taste

18 clams, well scrubbed

1 crab or lobster, cooked, cracked, and sectioned into 2–3-inch (5–7.5-cm) pieces

18 mussels, well scrubbed and debearded

18 shrimp (prawns), peeled and deveined

18 sea scallops, tough muscles removed

¼ cup (⅓ oz/10 g) chopped fresh parsley or basil

Sizzling Rice Cake Soup with Crab

½ cup (3½ oz/105 g) long-grain rice

½ cup (4 fl oz/125 ml) water

6 dried Chinese black mushrooms, soaked in warm water for 20 minutes, then drained

1 tablespoon peanut oil, plus oil for frying

1 teaspoon salt

4 water chestnuts, finely diced

½ cup (2½ oz/75 g) drained, canned bamboo shoots, finely diced

¼ cup (2 fl oz/60 ml) Chinese rice wine or dry sherry

6 cups (48 fl oz/1.5 l) chicken broth

1 tablespoon light soy sauce

Large pinch of ground white pepper

Large pinch of sugar

3 tablespoons cornstarch (cornflour) mixed with ¼ cup (2 fl oz/60 ml) water

½ cup (2½ oz/75 g) frozen petite peas, thawed

½ lb (250 g) firm tofu, finely diced

¼ lb (125 g) cooked fresh crabmeat, flaked

1 green (spring) onion, chopped

Place the rice in a fine-mesh sieve and rinse under cold running water until the water runs clear; drain thoroughly. In a small frying pan over medium-high heat, combine the rice and water and bring to a boil, stirring to loosen the grains from the pan bottom. Cook until the surface water is completely absorbed, about 5 minutes. Reduce the heat to low, cover, and cook until the rice is glistening white, about 15 minutes. Uncover and continue to cook until it shrinks from the pan sides and forms a hard crust, about 15 minutes. It should be easy to lift from the pan with a spatula; if not, continue to cook. Let cool, then break into 2-inch (5-cm) pieces.

Remove the stems from the mushrooms and discard. Finely dice the caps. Heat a large saucepan over medium-high heat. Add the 1 tablespoon oil, salt, mushrooms, water chestnuts, and bamboo shoots and toss and stir for 30 seconds. Pour in the rice wine or sherry and cook until the alcohol evaporates, about 15 seconds. Add the broth, soy sauce, white pepper, and sugar, stir well, and bring to a boil. Add the cornstarch mixture, stirring continuously, and cook until thickened, about 30 seconds. Remove from the heat, cover, and keep warm.

Preheat an oven to 425°F (220°C). Line a baking sheet with paper towels. In a saucepan over medium-high heat, pour oil to a depth of 2 inches (5 cm) and heat until 375°F (190°C) on a deep-frying thermometer. Working in batches, add the rice cakes to the hot oil. Fry until puffed and doubled in size, about 5 seconds. (If the rice cakes do not puff in the oil within 10 seconds, the oil is not hot enough or the cakes are not bone-dry.) Using tongs, turn and fry until golden, about 10 seconds. Transfer to the towel-lined baking sheet and keep warm in the oven. Just before the last batch is fried, bring the soup to a boil over high heat and add the peas and tofu. Transfer to a tureen and add the crabmeat and green onion.

Bring the soup to the table and immediately add the hot rice cakes. They should sizzle on contact. Ladle into bowls and serve at once.

Serves 6

New England Clam Chowder

The smoky taste of bacon or the sweetness of pancetta adds a more refined touch than the salt pork traditionally used in New England–style chowder. In the summer, you may want to add about 2 cups (12 oz/375 g) corn kernels with the clams.

In a large, wide saucepan over high heat, combine the clams and the wine, water, or stock. Cover and cook until the clams open, about 5 minutes. Using a slotted spoon, transfer the clams to a bowl, discarding any that did not open. Strain the cooking liquid through a sieve lined with damp cheesecloth (muslin) placed over a large bowl. Remove the clams from their shells and chop coarsely, capturing and straining any of the juices. Measure the cooking liquid and add enough clam juice or fish stock to measure 5 cups (40 fl oz/1.25 l). Set aside.

In a saucepan over medium-low heat, warm the olive oil. Add the pancetta or bacon and onions and cook, stirring occasionally to prevent sticking, until softened, about 10 minutes. Raise the heat to high, add the reserved liquid, and bring to a boil. Add the potatoes and reduce the heat to low. Cook, uncovered, until the potatoes are firm but almost completely cooked through, 10–15 minutes. Add the clams and simmer until heated through, about 4 minutes. Add the cream and season with the black pepper and the cayenne pepper, if using. Swirl in the butter, if using, and top with the chopped herbs.

Ladle into warmed individual bowls and serve immediately.

Serves 6

5 lb (2.5 kg) littleneck or cherrystone clams (48–60 clams), well scrubbed

About 2 cups (16 fl oz/500 ml) dry white wine, water, or fish stock

About 3 cups (24 fl oz/750 ml) bottled clam juice or fish stock

2 tablespoons olive oil

6 oz (185 g) pancetta or bacon, cut into small pieces

2 yellow onions, chopped

6–8 small red new potatoes, cut into small chunks

1$\frac{1}{2}$ cups (12 fl oz/375 ml) heavy (double) cream

Ground black pepper to taste

Pinch of cayenne pepper (optional)

2 tablespoons unsalted butter (optional)

$\frac{1}{4}$ cup ($\frac{1}{3}$ oz/10 g) chopped fresh parsley or chives, or 2 tablespoons chopped fresh thyme

Brazilian Shellfish Soup

1/4 cup (2 oz/60 g) butter

3 yellow onions, chopped

2 jalapeño chiles, minced

4 cloves garlic, minced

2 tablespoons peeled and grated fresh ginger

1 tablespoon ground coriander

4–5 cups (32–40 fl oz/1–1.25 l) fish stock

2 cups (12 oz/375 g) peeled, seeded, and chopped tomatoes

1/2 cup (4 fl oz/125 ml) coconut milk

1/4 teaspoon saffron threads, steeped in 1/4 cup (2 fl oz/60 ml) white wine

1/4 cup (1/3 oz/10 g) chopped fresh cilantro (fresh coriander)

2–3 tablespoons lime juice

Salt and ground pepper to taste

1 1/2 lb (750 g) firm white fish fillets, cut into chunks

18 *each* mussels, scrubbed and debearded; shrimp (prawns), shelled and deveined with tails intact; and sea scallops

About 6 cups (30 oz/940 g) hot, cooked white rice

3 tablespoons *each* chopped fresh cilantro (fresh coriander) and toasted shredded dried coconut

In a wide, deep saucepan over medium heat, melt the butter. Add the onions and sauté, stirring occasionally, until tender and translucent, about 10 minutes. Add the jalapeños, garlic, ginger, and coriander and sauté until heated through and the flavors are blended, about 5 minutes. Add the stock, tomatoes, coconut milk, saffron and wine, and cilantro and simmer for about 3 minutes to blend the flavors. Add the lime juice to taste, and season with salt and pepper. Taste and adjust the balance of sweet and sour flavors.

Add the white fish, mussels (discard any that do not close to the touch), and shrimp and simmer until the shrimp are pink, about 3 minutes. Add the scallops during the last 2 minutes and simmer just until the mussels open and the scallops are opaque throughout.

To serve, place 1 cup (5 oz/155 g) rice in each large warmed soup bowl. Ladle the soup into the bowls, dividing the shellfish as evenly as possible and discarding any mussels that did not open. Garnish with the cilantro and coconut. Serve hot.

Serves 6

Chicken, Tortilla, and Lime Soup

In this classic soup, called *sopa de lima*, from Mexico's Yucatán region, the chicken is not cooked directly in the stock because it will make it cloudy. Be careful not to add too much chile or the soup may be too fiery for comfort.

In a large saucepan over high heat, bring 3 1/2 quarts (3.5 l) of the broth to a boil. Reduce the heat so the broth boils gently and boil until reduced by half to about 7 cups (56 fl oz/1.75 l), about 30 minutes.

Meanwhile, pour vegetable oil into a deep frying pan to a depth of 2 inches (5 cm) and heat to 375°F (190°C) on a deep-frying thermometer. Working in batches, drop in the tortilla strips and fry until golden and crisp, about 2 minutes. Using a slotted spoon, transfer the fried tortilla strips to paper towels to drain.

In a saucepan, combine the chicken breasts with the remaining 2 cups (16 fl oz/500 ml) broth. Bring to a simmer and cook gently until the chicken is opaque throughout, about 8 minutes. Transfer to a cutting board and, when cool enough to handle, cut the chicken breasts into bite-sized pieces. Set aside. Discard the broth or reserve for another use. If not using immediately, cover and refrigerate.

In a large saucepan over medium heat, warm the olive oil. Add the onion and sauté, stirring occasionally, until tender and translucent, about 10 minutes. Add the garlic and jalapeño chile and cook for 1–2 minutes to soften. Add the reduced broth, raise the heat to high, and bring to a boil. Reduce the heat to low, add the cooked chicken, the tomatoes, cilantro, lime juice, salt, and pepper, and simmer until the chicken is heated through, about 5 minutes. Taste and adjust the seasonings.

Ladle the hot soup into warmed bowls. Sprinkle the lime pieces and tortilla strips evenly over the tops. Serve immediately.

Serves 6

4 quarts (4 l) chicken broth

Vegetable oil for deep-frying

3 corn tortillas, cut into strips 2 inches (5 cm) long

1 1/4 lb (625 g) boneless, skinless chicken breasts

3 tablespoons olive oil

1 large yellow onion, chopped

2 tablespoons minced garlic

2–3 teaspoons finely minced jalapeño chile, with or without seeds to taste

1 1/2 cups (9 oz/280 g) peeled, seeded, and diced tomatoes (fresh or canned)

6 tablespoons (1/4 oz/7 g) chopped fresh cilantro (fresh coriander)

6 tablespoons (3 fl oz/90 ml) fresh lime juice

1 1/2 teaspoons salt, or to taste

1/2 teaspoon ground pepper

12 paper-thin lime slices, cut into quarters

Chicken Coconut Soup with Lemongrass

This popular Thai soup is also know as *tom kha gai*. If you cannot find galangal (a gingerlike rhizome), fresh ginger works well in its place. Garnish with fresh cilantro (fresh coriander) leaves and thinly sliced small fresh red or green chiles.

4 cups (32 fl oz/1 l) chicken broth

8 large slices peeled fresh galangal or 4 slices peeled fresh ginger

1 large lemongrass stalk, cut into 2-inch (5-cm) pieces, crushed

16 fresh kaffir lime leaves, torn in half, or grated zest of 1 large lime

2 cans (14 fl oz/430 ml each) coconut milk

1/4 cup (2 fl oz/60 ml) lime or lemon juice

2–3 tablespoons Thai fish sauce

2 tablespoons light brown sugar

1 tablespoon red chile paste

1 lb (500 g) boneless, skinless chicken breasts, cut into bite-sized pieces

1/2 lb (250 g) fresh white mushrooms, brushed clean and thinly sliced

In a large saucepan, combine the broth, galangal or ginger, lemongrass, and lime leaves or lime zest. Place over medium heat and slowly bring to a boil. Boil for 1 minute.

Reduce the heat to low, add the coconut milk, stir to combine, and bring to a simmer. Add the lime or lemon juice, fish sauce, brown sugar, and chile paste; mix well, and simmer for 5 minutes. Add the chicken pieces and simmer until tender, 4–5 minutes. Add the mushrooms and simmer until tender, about 1 minute longer.

To serve, ladle into warmed bowls.

Serves 4–6

Chicken Noodle Soup

On a cold night, hot soup is the ultimate comfort food—especially when it's a nourishing bowl of chicken, vegetables, and egg noodles. Precede it with a salad of escarole (Batavian endive) and apples and follow with a selection of cookies.

In a soup pot over medium heat, combine the chicken and water. Bring to a simmer, skimming off any foam that forms on the surface. Add the onion, and parsley and bay leaf, adjust the heat to maintain a gentle simmer, and cook, uncovered, for 20 minutes. Add the carrots and celery and continue to simmer gently, uncovered, until the broth is flavorful, about 40 minutes longer.

Using tongs or a slotted spoon, remove and discard the onion, cloves, and parsley and bay leaf. Transfer the chicken pieces to a cutting board. If using chicken wings, cut off and discard the wing tips. When cool enough to handle, skin and remove the meat from the remaining pieces. Return the meat to the broth. Season the soup with salt and pepper.

Bring a large pot three-fourths full of salted water to a boil over high heat. Add the noodles and cook until slightly underdone, about 10 minutes or according to package directions. Drain and transfer to the soup, then simmer gently for 1 minute to blend the flavors.

Ladle into warm bowls and serve hot.

Makes 6 servings

12 chicken wings or 2½ lbs (1.25 kg) assorted bony chicken parts, such as wings, backs, thighs, and/or drumsticks

12 cups (3 qts/3 l) cold water, or a combination of chicken broth and water

1 large yellow onion stuck with 2 whole cloves and cut in half

6 fresh parsley sprigs tied together with 1 bay leaf

3 carrots, peeled and sliced or diced, if large

3 celery ribs, sliced or diced

Salt and ground pepper to taste

6 oz (185 g) dried egg noodles, broken into 3-inch lengths

Meatball Soup

FOR THE MEATBALLS

1/2 lb (250 g) ground (minced) beef, veal, or lamb

1/2 cup (1 oz/30 g) fresh bread crumbs

1/4 cup (1 1/2 oz/45 g) grated yellow onion

1 egg

1/4 cup (1/3 oz/10 g) chopped fresh flat-leaf (Italian) parsley

1 clove garlic, finely minced (optional)

Salt and ground pepper to taste

1 teaspoon vegetable oil

FOR THE SOUP BASE

2 tablespoons olive oil

1 1/2 cups (6 oz/185 g) chopped yellow onion

8 cups (64 fl oz/2 l) beef broth

2–3 cups (16–24 fl oz/500–750 ml) canned tomato purée

3 cups (1 1/4 lb/625 g) cooked chopped greens such as escarole or chard (optional)

Salt and ground pepper to taste

1/4 cup (1/3 oz/10 g) chopped fresh flat-leaf (Italian) parsley (optional)

To make the meatballs, in a bowl, combine the meat, bread crumbs, onion, egg, parsley, and garlic (if using). Mix well, then season with salt and pepper. In a small frying pan, heat the 1 teaspoon of oil over medium-high heat. When hot, fry a tiny nugget of the mixture until cooked through, taste, and adjust the seasonings if needed. Line a large baking sheet with parchment (baking) paper. Form the meat mixture into tiny meatballs about the size of a marble and place on the prepared baking sheet in a single layer. Cover and refrigerate until ready to cook.

To make the soup base, in a large saucepan over medium heat, warm the 2 tablespoons olive oil. Add the onion and sauté, stirring occasionally, until tender and translucent, about 10 minutes. Raise the heat to high and add the broth and tomato purée and bring to a boil. Reduce the heat to low and simmer for 10 minutes.

Gently slip the meatballs into the soup base and simmer over low heat until the meatballs are cooked through and tender, about 20 minutes. Add the the cooked greens, if using, and simmer until heated through, about 5 minutes longer. Taste and adjust the seasonings.

Ladle into warmed bowls and garnish with the parsley, if desired. Serve immediately.

Serves 6

Beef Barley Soup

A garnish of sour cream and chopped dill gives this hearty soup a Russian flavor. Serve with dark rye bread and a salad of crisp greens for a complete meal. It can be made a day or two ahead—let cool, cover, and refrigerate, then reheat before serving.

Place the shanks in a saucepan and add water to cover generously. Bring to a boil over high heat, skimming often to remove any foam that forms on the surface. Add about two-thirds of the chopped onions, the carrots, and the celery, reduce the heat to low, and cook, uncovered, for about 1 hour. Add the tomato purée and the barley, cover partially, and continue to cook over low heat until the barley is tender, about 1 hour longer.

While the soup is cooking, in a large sauté pan over medium heat, melt the butter. Add the remaining chopped onions and sauté, stirring occasionally, until pale gold, 10–12 minutes. Raise the heat to high, add the mushrooms, and sauté, stirring often, until softened, 6–8 minutes. Add the garlic, reduce the heat to medium, and sauté until soft but not brown, about 3 minutes longer. Season with salt, pepper, and 2 tablespoons of the dill.

Remove the shanks from the pan and, when cool enough to handle, cut the meat from the bone. Chop and reserve the meat; you should have about $1^1/_3$ cups (8 oz/250 g).

Add the mushroom mixture and the reserved beef to the pan and stir to heat through. Season with salt and pepper.

Ladle into warmed bowls and sprinkle with the remaining 2 tablespoons dill and the parsley. Top each serving with a dollop of sour cream, if desired.

Serves 6

3 lb (1.5 kg) meaty beef or veal shanks

3 large yellow onions, chopped

6 carrots, peeled and chopped

4 celery stalks, chopped

1 cup (8 fl oz/250 ml) tomato purée

1 cup (8 oz/250 g) barley

6 tablespoons (3 oz/90 g) unsalted butter

1 lb (500 g) fresh cremini mushrooms, brushed clean and sliced

$^1/_2$ teaspoon minced garlic

Salt and ground pepper to taste

4 tablespoons ($^1/_3$ oz/10 g) chopped fresh dill

$^1/_4$ cup ($^1/_3$ oz/10 g) chopped fresh flat-leaf (Italian) parsley

6 tablespoons (3 fl oz/90 ml) sour cream (optional)

Pork and Nopales Stew with Purslane and Cilantro

Nopales, or cactus pads, have a delightful citruslike flavor and a smooth texture. Purslane also has a slight citrus flavor. If you cannot find purslane, omit it, as there is no good substitute. Choose nopales that are bright green, firm, and free of mold.

2 lb (1 kg) lean pork butt or shoulder, cut into 2-inch (5-cm) cubes

2 teaspoons salt

4–6 pasilla chiles

$1^{1}/_{2}$–2 cups (12–16 fl oz/375–500 ml) boiling water

3 jalapeño chiles, seeded and chopped

1 large yellow onion, chopped

4 cloves garlic, chopped

1 piece fresh ginger, about 2 inches (5 cm), peeled and chopped

1 teaspoon ground pepper

$1^{1}/_{2}$ lb (750 g) tomatoes, peeled, seeded, and chopped (see technique, page 291)

2 cups (16 fl oz/500 ml) chicken broth

1 large nopal cactus pad

1 cup (1 oz/30 g) fresh purslane leaves

$^{1}/_{4}$ cup ($^{1}/_{4}$ oz/7 g) fresh cilantro (fresh coriander) leaves

In a heavy-bottomed saucepan, combine the pork with water to cover by 2 inches (5 cm). Add 1 teaspoon of the salt and bring to a boil over high heat. Reduce the heat to low, cover, and simmer until the pork is tender, $1^{1}/_{2}$–2 hours.

Meanwhile, place a frying pan over medium-high heat. Place the pasilla chiles in the pan and toast, turning once, until fragrant and lightly browned, about 1 minute on each side. Transfer to a heatproof bowl and pour in enough boiling water to cover fully. Let stand for 30 minutes. Remove from the water (reserve the soaking water), discard the skins and seeds, and coarsely chop the chiles. In a blender or food processor, combine the pasillas, jalapeños, onion, garlic, ginger, pepper, and 3 or 4 tablespoons of the reserved soaking water. Purée until a medium-thick paste forms, adding more water if necessary to achieve the correct consistency. Set aside.

When the pork is ready, drain it and place in a clean saucepan. Add the chile mixture, tomatoes, and chicken broth. Bring to a boil over high heat, reduce the heat to low, and simmer, uncovered, until fork-tender, about 45 minutes.

If the thorns have not been removed from the cactus pad, hold it with tongs and scrape away the thorns with a sharp knife. Peel off the skin, starting at the outer edges. Cut the pad into $^{1}/_{2}$-inch (12-mm) squares. (The stew can be made ahead to this point. Cover and refrigerate for up to 24 hours.)

Add the cactus and purslane to the pork and cook until tender and easily pierced with a knife, 20–30 minutes longer. Garnish with the cilantro and serve at once.

Serves 6

Basic Recipes & Techniques

These basic recipes and techniques are used throughout this book. Once you have mastered them, you'll turn to them again and again to create delicious recipes.

Chicken Stock

Any type of chicken can be used for making this stock, although pieces of a stewing chicken (usually a more mature bird) will yield the most flavor.

6 lb (3 kg) chicken parts such as necks, backs, wings, and thighs

2 yellow onions, coarsely chopped

2 small carrots, coarsely chopped

1 large celery stalk, chopped

green tops of 2 leeks, chopped (optional)

2 cloves garlic

2 or 3 fresh parsley sprigs

6–8 peppercorns

2 or 3 fresh thyme sprigs

2 small bay leaves

Rinse the chicken parts, place in a stockpot, and add water to cover by 3 inches (7.5 cm). Bring to a boil, reduce the heat to low, and skim off any scum from the surface. Simmer, uncovered, for 1 hour, skimming as needed.

Add all the remaining ingredients, cover partially, and simmer gently for about 4 hours. Remove from the heat.

Scoop out and discard the solids, then pour through a fine-mesh sieve lined with damp cheesecloth (muslin) into 1 or more storage containers. Refrigerate, uncovered, until well chilled and the fat has solidified on top. Lift off and discard the fat. Use the stock at this point or cover and refrigerate for up to 5 days or freeze for up to 3 months.

Makes about 4 qt (4 l)

Vegetable Stock

Roasting the vegetables before adding water gives this particular stock a special depth of flavor.

5 carrots, cut into chunks

3 leeks, cut into chunks

3 celery stalks, cut into chunks

2 yellow onions, quartered

1 red (Spanish) onion, quartered

1 head garlic, halved

2 fresh thyme sprigs

1 bay leaf

5 peppercorns

4 qt (4 l) water

Preheat an oven to 450°F (230°C).

Place the carrots, leeks, celery, yellow and red onions, and garlic in a roasting pan. Roast, uncovered, stirring occasionally, until well browned, about 1 hour.

Transfer the vegetables to a stockpot. Add the thyme sprigs, bay leaf, and peppercorns, and then pour in the water. Bring to a boil over high heat, cover, reduce the heat to low, and simmer for 1 hour.

Remove from the heat. Strain through a fine-mesh sieve lined with damp cheesecloth (muslin). Use the stock at this point or transfer to 1 or more storage containers. Refrigerate, uncovered, until cold, then cover and refrigerate for up to 1 week or freeze for up to 3 months.

Makes 3 1/2–4 qt (3.5–4 l)

Beef Stock

Making stock at home is an all-day task, but the results are well worth the effort. You can prepare a large batch of stock and freeze it in small containers for future use.

6 lb (3 kg) meaty beef shanks, cracked

1 marrowbone, cracked

2 yellow onions, chopped

2 carrots, chopped

1 celery stalk, chopped

1 leek, chopped (optional)

2 cups (16 fl oz/500 ml) water

2 tomatoes, halved

6 cloves garlic

5 fresh parsley sprigs

2 small bay leaves

3 fresh thyme sprigs

8 peppercorns

2 whole cloves

Mushroom stems (optional)

Preheat an oven to 450°F (230°C). Place the shanks and marrowbone in a roasting pan. Roast, turning occasionally, until browned, about 1 1/2 hours. Transfer to a stockpot, but do not clean the roasting pan. Add water to cover the bones by 4 inches (10 cm) and bring to a boil, skimming often. Reduce the heat to low and simmer, uncovered, for 1–2 hours, skimming occasionally.

Meanwhile, brown the onions, carrots, celery, and leek (if using) in the roasting pan over medium-high heat until caramelized, 15–20 minutes. Add to the stockpot. Pour the water into the roasting pan and deglaze over medium-high heat, stirring to remove any browned bits from the pan bottom. Set aside.

When the shanks have simmered for 1–2 hours, add the deglazed juices to the stockpot along with all the remaining ingredients. Cover partially and simmer gently for at least 4 hours or up to 8 hours.

Remove from the heat. Scoop out and discard all the solids, then pour through a fine-mesh sieve lined with damp cheesecloth (muslin) into 1 or more storage containers. Refrigerate, uncovered, until well chilled and the fat has solidified on top. Lift off and discard the fat. Use the stock at this point or cover and refrigerate for up to 4 days or freeze for up to 3 months.

Makes about 4 qt (4 l)

Fish Stock

Homemade fish stock offers subtle flavor to seafood soups. Good-quality frozen fish stock is also available in specialty food shops. Bottled clam juice, either on its own or mixed with chicken broth, can also be substituted.

2 tablespoons olive oil

4 lb (2 kg) fish frames from mild fish, including heads and tails but gills removed, rinsed under cold water

2 cups (16 fl oz/500 ml) dry white wine

2 or 3 yellow onions, coarsely chopped

3 celery stalks, coarsely chopped

2 lemon zest strips

3 fresh parsley sprigs

2 fresh thyme sprigs

5–8 peppercorns

3 whole coriander seeds

2 whole allspice

1 small bay leaf

1 walnut-sized piece fresh ginger, peeled (optional) and lightly crushed

6 cups (48 fl oz/1.5 l) water, or as needed

In a stockpot over medium heat, warm the oil. Add the fish frames and sauté, stirring often, until they give off a little liquid, about 10 minutes. Add all the remaining ingredients including water as needed to immerse the bones. Bring to a boil, skim off any scum, reduce the heat to low, and simmer, uncovered, for 30 minutes, skimming often.

Remove from the heat and strain through a fine-mesh sieve lined with damp cheesecloth (muslin). Use the stock at this point or transfer to a container. Refrigerate, uncovered, until cold, then cover and refrigerate for up to 2 days or freeze for up to 3 months.

Makes about 8 cups (64 fl oz/2 l)

Bouquet Garni

1 bay leaf

6 whole peppercorns

1 clove garlic, sliced

3 fresh flat-leaf (Italian) parsley sprigs

Cut out a 6-inch (15-cm) square of the cheesecloth (muslin). Place the bay leaf, peppercorns, garlic, and parsley sprigs in the center of the cheesecloth, bring the corners together, and tie securely with kitchen string. Use as directed in individual recipes.

Makes 1 sachet

Garlic-Lime Dipping Sauce

1/4 cup (2 oz/60 g) sugar

1/4 cup (2 fl oz/60 ml) hot water

1 red serrano chile

2 cloves garlic, chopped

1/3 cup (3 fl oz/80 ml) lime juice

1/4 cup (2 fl oz/60 ml) fish sauce

In a bowl, combine the sugar and hot water, stirring to dissolve the sugar. Seed and finely chop the serrano chile. Add to the sauce with the garlic, lime juice, and fish sauce.

Makes about 1 cup (8 fl oz/250 ml)

Indian Green Chutney

3 cups (3 oz/90 g) fresh cilantro (fresh coriander) leaves

1/4 cup (1/4 oz/7 g) fresh mint leaves

1–3 serrano chiles, seeded and coarsely chopped

1 piece fresh ginger, 1 inch (12 mm), peeled and coarsely chopped

1 clove garlic

1/2 cup (4 fl oz/125 ml) water

Juice of 1/2 lime

1 teaspoon sugar, or to taste

Salt to taste

In a blender or food processor, combine the cilantro, mint, chiles, ginger, garlic, water, lime juice, sugar, and salt to taste. Purée until smooth. Add more water if needed to achieve a good consistency. Taste and adjust the seasonings.

Makes 1 1/4 cups (10 fl oz/310 ml)

Pesto

1/4 cup (2 oz/60 g) lightly toasted pine nuts or walnuts

2 cups (3 oz/90 g) tightly packed fresh basil leaves

2 or 3 cloves garlic

1/2 cup (1 oz/30 g) grated pecorino sardo or Parmesan cheese

1/2 cup (4 fl oz/125 ml) extra-virgin olive oil, or as needed

Salt and ground pepper to taste

In a food processor, combine the nuts, basil, and garlic. Pulse until the basil is chopped. Add the cheese and pulse to combine. With the motor running, pour in the 1/2 cup (4 fl oz/125 ml) oil, a few drops at a time, until the mixture has the consistency of mayonnaise, adding more oil as needed. Season with salt and pepper.

Makes about 1 1/2 cups (12 fl oz/180 ml)

Croutons

1 baguette, cut into small cubes

3 tablespoons olive oil

1 clove garlic, cut in half

1/2 cup (2 oz/60 g) Parmesan

Preheat an oven to 425°F (220°C). Arrange the bread cubes on a baking sheet and toast until golden, about 7 minutes. In a large sauté pan over medium-high heat, warm the olive oil. Add the garlic and sauté until lightly browned, about 4 minutes. Discard the garlic. Working in batches, sauté the bread cubes, tossing constantly, until browned and crisp, about 5 minutes. Transfer to paper towels to drain, then sprinkle with the Parmesan.

Makes about 4 cups (6 oz/180 g)

Red Pepper Cream

2 large red bell peppers (capsicums)

2 tablespoons fresh oregano leaves

2 tablespoons medium-hot pure ground chile such as pasilla or 1 tablespoon cayenne pepper

1 tablespoon olive oil

1/2 teaspoon salt

2 tablespoons heavy (double) cream

Preheat a broiler (griller). Halve and seed the bell peppers and place, cut sides down, on a broiler pan. Broil (grill) about 4 inches (10 cm) from the heat source until the skins are blackened and blistered. Remove from the broiler, drape the peppers loosely with aluminum foil, and let stand for 10 minutes, then peel away the skins. Place the peppers in a blender. Add the oregano, ground chile or cayenne, olive oil, and salt. Purée the mixture, drizzling in the cream.

Makes about 2/3 cup (5 fl oz/ 160 ml)

Rolling Sushi

1. With moistened hands, spread rice on a lightly toasted nori sheet aligned on a bamboo sushi mat. Arrange the filling in an even horizontal strip across the rice. Lift the nearest edge of mat, nori, and rice over the filling to seal it inside.

2. Continue to lift and press on the mat to form a snug roll. Pull back on the mat as you push and roll the nori and rice away from you.

Shucking Oysters

1. Scrub the shell with a stiff-bristled brush under cold running water. Using a folded kitchen towel, grip an oyster, flat side up. Push in an oyster knife to one side of the hinge and pry upward.

2. Keeping the blade edge against the inside of the top shell, run the knife all around to sever the muscle holding the halves together. Cut beneath the oyster to detach it from the bottom shell.

 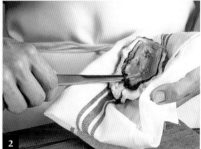

Peeling Tomatoes

1. Bring a pot of water to a boil. Fill a bowl with ice water. Immerse cored tomatoes in boiling water for 30 seconds, then transfer to the ice water.

2. When the tomatoes have cooled, peel off the loosened skins. If seeding is desired, halve the tomatoes horizontally and squeeze out the seed sacs.

Glossary

Arugula Green leaf vegetable, Mediterranean in origin, with slender, multiple-lobed leaves that have a peppery, slightly bitter flavor. Often used raw in salads; also known as rocket.

Asian Sesame Oil This amber-colored oil, pressed from toasted sesame seeds, has a rich, nutty flavor. Look for it in well-stocked markets and Asian groceries.

Bread Crumbs Fresh or dried bread crumbs are sometimes used to add body and texture to a variety of dishes. Panko are coarse commercially-made Japanese bread crumbs. Fine dried bread crumbs are also sold prepackaged in markets.

TO MAKE BREAD CRUMBS
Choose a good-quality, rustic-style loaf made of unbleached wheat flour, with a firm, coarse-textured crumb. For fresh crumbs, cut away the crusts and crumble the bread by hand into a blender or food processor fitted with the metal blade. For dried crumbs, proceed as for fresh crumbs through crumbling by hand or machine, then spread the crumbs on a baking pan. Dry slowly, about 1 hour, in an oven set at its lowest temperature.

Bonito Flakes Known in Japanese as *katsuobushi*, these almost transparent shavings are cut from blocks of dried bonito fish. Valued as a flavoring for broth and sauces and as a garnish, the flakes have a heady taste and scent somewhat reminiscent of smoked bacon. The shavings are sold already cut and packaged in cellophane; look for those with pale color and good aroma.

Chickpeas Chickpeas (garbanzo beans) are readily available canned, but are also available dried or ground to a flour in well-stocked markets or those that specialize in Middle Eastern or Indian ingredients. Chickpea flour, also known as garbanzo flour, is the ground form of dried chickpeas. It is used as a thickener for some curry sauces. You'll find it in most Italian delis, as well as in Indian markets (labeled *channa del flour*) and in Middle Eastern stores (labeled *besan*).

Chile Paste Cooks in Southeast Asia make use of pastes that combine roasted fresh or dried chiles with a variety of other seasonings, such as garlic, shallots, dried shrimp paste, tamarind water, and palm sugar. Various commercial chile pastes are sold.

Chorizo Sausage Coarsely ground spicy pork sausage used in Mexican and Spanish cooking. It's best to remove the casings before cooking.

Fennel The stems of a fennel plant swell to overlap the base, forming a bulb with white to pale green ribbed layers that look similar to celery. Fennel is known for its mild anise flavor.

Fish Sauce A liquid used in Southeast Asian cooking and as a table condiment, much like soy sauce. It ranges in color from amber to dark brown and has a pungent aroma and strong salty flavor. Although it varies slightly from country to country, all fish sauces are interchangeable. The most commonly available varieties are Thai fish sauce (*nam pla*) and Vietnamese fish sauce (*nuoc mam*).

Frisée A close relative of chicory (curly endive) but with a more delicate flavor and slightly more tender leaves. The pale green leaves with spiky edges form a loose head.

Galangal Similar in appearance to ginger, to which it is related, this gnarled rhizome adds a mustardlike, slightly medicinal flavor to simmered dishes. Known in Thailand as *kha*, in Indonesia and Malaysia as *laos*, and sometimes also referred to in English as Siamese ginger, galangal is available fresh and frozen whole and as dried slices. If only the dried form can be found, use half the quantity you would for fresh. If dried galangal will be pounded or blended, reconstitute it first by soaking in warm water for 30 minutes until pliable. For some soups and curries, the unsoaked pieces can be added directly to the simmering liquid.

Garam Masala A common Indian household seasoning blend that differs from region to region but which may include such dried ground spices as cloves, cardamom, cinnamon, coriander, cumin, fennel, fenugreek, ginger, and turmeric. Available in Indian markets and in the spice or specialty-food sections of well-stocked markets. It can also be made at home.

TO MAKE GARAM MASALA
Combine 1 cinnamon stick, 4 whole cloves, seeds from 5 cardamom pods, and 1 tablespoon *each* cumin seeds, coriander seeds, and peppercorns in a dry nonstick frying pan over medium heat. Toast, shaking the pan occasionally, until aromatic and darkened slightly, about 5 minutes. Let cool, then grind in a spice mill to a fine consistency. Store in a tightly sealed jar at room temperature for up to 6 months.

Ginger A refreshing combination of spicy and sweet in both aroma and flavor, ginger adds a lively note to many recipes, particularly Asian dishes. Select ginger that is firm and heavy and has a smooth skin.

Jerusalem Artichokes These tuberous vegetables, which resemble small potatoes, get their name in part

Cheese

A good cheese shop is a rewarding experience, since you'll be able to taste a variety of types before you buy. Store cheeses in a warmer part of the refrigerator, wrapped in parchment (baking) or waxed paper rather than plastic, to allow them to breathe.

Goat Sharply tangy goat cheeses, also known by the generic French term *chèvre*, are made in innumerable varieties. The types of goat cheese most commonly available are fresh and creamy and are usually sold in small rounds or logs.

Feta A young cheese traditionally made from sheep's milk and known for its crumbly texture. Feta's saltiness is heightened by the brine in which the cheese is packed.

Fromage Blanc A mild, fresh cheese made from skim or whole milk, with or without cream added. It is eaten flavored with sugar as a simple dessert and also used in cooking.

Goat Made from pure goat's milk, or a blend of goat's and cow's milk, fresh goat cheese is creamy and tangy. Montrachet, a well-known variety is soft and spreadable.

Italian Fontinella This cheese is a mild and creamy semi-hard cheese. Its flavor is reminiscent of Provolone but is less sharp.

Kefalotiri Popular Greek sheep's milk cheese, most commonly aged until hard and yellow.

Mozzarella This rindless Italian white cheese has a mild taste and soft but dense texture. Mozzarella made in the traditional way from water buffalo's milk may be found fresh, immersed in water, in well-stocked food stores. If only packaged cow's milk mozzarella, which tends to be drier and less flavorful, is available, look for balls sold in water rather than dry-packed in plastic.

Parmesan This firm, aged, salty cheese is made from partially skimmed cow's milk. Seek out imported Parmigiano-Reggiano, which has a rich, nutty flavor and a pleasant, granular texture; it is the most renowned of all Parmesan cheeses.

Pecorino Italian sheep's milk cheese, sold either fresh or aged. Two of its most popular aged forms are *pecorino romano* and *pecorino sardo*; the latter cheese is tangier than the former.

Roquefort This sheep's milk cheese comes from France with a moist, crumbly interior and a true, clean, strong flavor. Some varieties are rather salty.

Chiles

Fresh chiles range in size from tiny to large, and in heat intensity from mild to fiery hot. Select firm, bright-colored chiles with blemish-free skins. To reduce the heat of a chile, remove the ribs and seeds (see below).

Anaheim Large, slender green chile about 6 inches (15 cm) long and 2 inches (5 cm) wide. Mild to slightly hot, they are also sometimes called long green or California chiles and are similar to, but somewhat milder than, New Mexican chiles. Roasted and peeled Anaheims are also widely available canned in most grocery stores.

Chipotle Dried and smoked jalapeños, with lots of flavor and lots of heat. These dark brown chiles are about 3 inches (7.5 cm) long and are sold either dried whole or ground.

Jalapeño Fresh torpedo-shaped chile (at right, top) usually measuring 2–4 inches (5–10 cm) long and ranging from mildly hot to fiery. Most often available green, but can also be red in color.

Pasilla Dark green to black chile when fresh and dark brown when dried. Moderately hot and with a hint of berry flavor. In fresh form sometimes labeled *chilaca*.

Poblano Large and fairly mild, the fresh, dark green poblano is about 5 inches (13 cm) long and has broad "shoulders." Poblano chiles, which are usually roasted and peeled, have a nutty flavor. When dried, these chiles are called ancho chiles.

Serrano Similar to a jalapeño chile in heat intensity, the serrano chile (left, bottom) is sleeker and tends to have more consistent heat than its cousin. About 2 inches (5 cm) long, serranos can be found in green or red form (the red ones are ripe versions of the green) and can be used in place of jalapeños in any recipe.

CAUTION Wear gloves when working with hot chiles to prevent burns to your fingers. The heat of chiles and their seeds can linger for several hours on your skin, so thoroughly was your hands, the cutting board, and the knife with hot soapy water as soon as you have finished working with the chiles. Be sure to avoid touching your face, especially your eyes and lips, and any other sensitive areas of your skin before you complete this thorough washing process.

because their flavor resembles an artichoke and in part because of their botanical kinship to the sunflower, *girasole* in Italian. They are at their best and most abundant in farmers' markets during winter.

Leeks Sweet, moderately flavored member of the onion family, long and cylindrical in shape with a pale white root end and dark green leaves. Select firm, unblemished leeks, small to medium in size. Grown in sandy soil, the leafy-topped, multi-layered vegetables require thorough cleaning.

TO CLEAN LEEKS
Trim off the tough ends of the dark green leaves. Trim off the roots. If a recipe calls for leek whites only, trim off the dark green leaves where they meet the slender pale-green part of the stem. Starting about 1 inch (2.5 cm) from the root end, slit the leek lengthwise. Vigorously swish the leek in a basin or sink filled with cold water. Drain and rinse again; check to make sure that no dirt remains between the tightly packed pale portion of the leaves.

Lemongrass An aromatic herb used in much of Southeast Asia, lemongrass resembles a green (spring) onion in shape but has a fresh lemony aroma and flavor. Use only the pale green bottom part for cooking. Since the fibers are tough, lemongrass needs to be removed from a dish after cooking much like a bay leaf.

Mussels Before cooking, these popular, bluish black-shelled bivalves may require special cleaning to remove any dirt adhering to their shells and to remove their "beards," the fibrous threads by which the mussels connect to rocks or piers in the coastal waters where they live.

TO CLEAN & DEBEARD MUSSELS Rinse the mussels thoroughly under cold running water. One at a time, hold them under the water and scrub with a firm-bristled brush to remove any stubborn dirt. Firmly grasp the fibrous beard attached to the side of each mussel and pull it off. Discard any mussels whose shells are not tightly closed.

Mirin A sweet Japanese cooking wine made by fermenting glutinous rice and sugar. The pale golden wine adds a rich flavor when added to a dish or dipping sauce.

Olives Olives are cured in both their unripe green and ripened brownish to black forms, using various combinations of salt, seasonings, brines, vinegars, and oils. Many types of cured olives are commonly available in grocery stores.

Herbs

Using fresh herbs is one of the best things you can do to improve your cooking. Dried herbs do have their place, but fresh herbs usually bring brighter flavors to a dish.

Basil and Opal Basil This sweet, spicy, tender-leafed herb goes especially well with tomatoes. Special basil varieties are found in well-stocked food stores and farmers' markets, including purple-leafed opal basil, which has a more pronounced flavor.

Chives These slender, hollow, grass-shaped blades give an onion-like flavor to dishes, without the bite.

Cilantro Also called fresh coriander or Chinese parsley, cilantro has a bright astringent taste. It is used extensively in Mexican, Asian, Indian, Latin, and Middle Eastern cuisines.

Dill This herb has fine, feathery leaves with a distinct aroma and flavor.

Flat-leaf (Italian) Parsley A dark green Italian variety of the faintly peppery herb, flat-leaf parsley adds vibrant color and a pleasing flavor to a wide variety of preparations.

Marjoram This Mediterranean herb, which has a milder flavor than

its close relative, oregano, is used best fresh. Pair it with tomatoes, eggplant, beans, poultry, and seafood.

Rosemary This woody Mediterranean herb with leaves like pine needles, has an assertive flavor. Always use rosemary in moderation, as its flavor can overwhelm a dish if you use too much of it.

Sage Soft, gray-green sage leaves are sweet and aromatic. Used fresh or dried, they pair with poultry, vegetables, and fresh or cured pork.

Tarragon With its distinctively reminiscent of anise, tarragon is used to season many salads and egg and vegetable dishes, as well as mild-tasting main-course ingredients such as chicken and fish.

Thyme A brightly flavored ancient herb of the eastern Mediterranean, thyme may be used fresh or dried. The variety known as lemon thyme has a distinctively citrusy taste that makes it a popular seasoning for seafood. Thyme is also a popular addition to roast poultry dishes.

Kalamata Pungent, brine-cured black variety with a thick almond shape.

Brine-cured green olives Olives picked in their unripened, green state and cured in brine—sometimes with seasonings, vinegars, and oils—to produce results generally more sharp tasting than ripe black olives.

Spanish olives Large, green, dense olives, often pitted and stuffed with pimientos, almonds, or anchovies.

Palm Sugar Derived from the sap of the coconut or other palms, and sometimes called coconut sugar, palm sugar is prized in Indonesia, Malaysia, and Thailand for its fragrant, caramel-like flavor and dark brown color. Vietnamese cooks use a lighter, milder version. Light or dark brown sugar, depending upon the color desired, can be substituted, although the flavor will not be the same.

Pita Bread This flat, round bread comes from the Middle East and is made with white or wheat flour and very little leavening. Known also as pocket bread or pita pockets, the bread forms a large hollow at the center as it bakes.

Rice Paper Rounds Made from rice flour and water, tissue-thin rice paper, indispensable to the Vietnamese pantry, is commonly purchased rather than made at home. It comes dried in both rounds and triangles of different sizes, with 8-inch (20-cm) rounds the most common. Before use, it must be made soft and pliable by dampening it with water (or another liquid), either by dipping it briefly in a bowl of water or by brushing it with water.

Rice Stick Noodles Thin rice vermicelli and ribbon-shaped rice sticks, particular specialties of Southeast Asia, are made from pre-cooked rice. The vermicelli need no cooking—only soaking in water until soft; thicker rice sticks may require boiling until tender.

Saffron An intensely aromatic spice, golden orange in color, made from the dried stigmas of a species of crocus; used to perfume and color many classic Mediterranean and East Indian dishes. Sold either as threads—the dried stigmas—or in powdered form. Look for products labeled pure saffron.

Seaweed The ocean yields this foodstuff, rich in nutrients and tasting of the sea, which is widely used in Asian cooking. The Japanese use more kinds of seaweed than any other culture, beginning with the nori used in making sushi. Dried nori, like many other seaweeds, is available in Japanese markets, most natural-food stores, and some supermarkets. It comes in dark green, dark brown, or black thin sheets that are either toasted or untoasted. Dark brown to grayish black kombu is kelp that is dried, cut, and folded. It is often mixed with dried bonito flakes as an ingredient in dashi, the typical Japanese stock.

Shrimp Although often sold peeled and deveined, it's best to purchase shrimp (prawns) still in their shells if possible. Most shrimp have been previously frozen, and the shells help preserve their texture and flavor.

TO PEEL & DEVEIN SHRIMP Using your thumbs, split open the shrimp's thin shell along the concave side, between its two rows of legs. Grasp the shell and gently peel it away. Using a small knife, make a shallow slit along the peeled shrimp's back, just deep enough to expose the long, usually dark, veinlike intestinal tract. With the tip of the knife or your fingers, lift up and pull out the vein, then discard it.

Sriracha Sauce Named for the seaside Thai town in which it originated, this bottled, hot or mild, sweet-tart all-purpose sauce is made from red chiles and resembles a light-colored ketchup. Keep in mind that even the so-called mild Sriracha is quite hot.

Tofu Also known as bean curd. Soft, custardlike curd, made from the milky liquid extracted from fresh soybeans, caused to solidify by a coagulating agent. Popular throughout Asia, both firm and soft fresh bean curd is widely available in Asian markets as well as in some food stores.

Tomatillos Once the loose, brown, papery husks of fresh tomatillos have been thrown away, the small green fruits inside closely resemble green tomatoes, although they are in fact related to the Cape gooseberry. Like tomatoes, however, tomatillos are used exclusively as a vegetable, contributing their tart, astringent flavor to both fresh and cooked sauces, particularly in Mexican cooking. Most well-stocked food stores also carry husked and peeled tomatillos in cans.

Watercress Refreshing, slightly peppery, dark green leaf vegetable commercially cultivated and also found wild in freshwater streams. Used primarily in salads and as a popular garnish.

Wasabi Powder Ground to a fine powder from a dried variety of powerful green horseradish, this Japanese seasoning is usually reconstituted with a little water to form a smooth paste that is used to flavor sushi and dipping sauces.

Mushrooms

The popularity of all types of mushrooms has resulted in the successful farming of many different varieties, blurring the distinction between cultivated and wild. Wild or farmed, mushrooms are delicious when roasted or grilled and contribute a deep earthiness to recipes.

White The cultivated, all-purpose mushroom sold in grocery stores. Sometimes called button mushrooms, although the term refers specifically to young, tender ones with closed caps. For general cooking, use the medium-sized mushrooms with little or no gills showing. The large ones are excellent for stuffing.

Cremini Closely related to the white mushroom and can be used whenever white mushrooms are called for, but they have a light brown color, firmer texture, and fuller flavor.

Morel Considered the king of all mushrooms, the morel has a strong, intense, musky flavor that makes it highly sought after. The uncultivated mushroom has a dark, elongated, spongelike cap and hollow stem. Morels are especially delicious in cream sauces and scrambled eggs, and typically used in French cuisine.

Oyster Cream to pale gray, these mushrooms have a fan shape and a subtle flavor of shellfish. They used to be wild only but are now cultivated.

Porcini Also known by the French term, cèpes. Porcini (Italian for "little pigs") are indeed nicely plump, with a firm texture, sweet fragrance, and full, earthy flavor. An uncultivated variety, they have caps similar to that of cremini in shape and color, but their stems are thick and swollen. They can be difficult to find in the U.S., however, dried porcini can be used. They are excellent in soups, pasta sauces, and risotto. Thinly slice young, fresh ones and dress them with a simple vinaigrette.

Portobello A cultivated mushroom, the portobello is a mature cremini mushroom. They have a smoky flavor and meaty texture. The thick, tough stems should be removed before cooking.

Shiitake The most popular mushroom in Japan is now widely cultivated. Buff to dark brown, they are available fresh and dried. Fresh shiitakes should have smooth, plump caps, while better-quality dried ones have pale cracks in the caps' surfaces. Dried shiitake and Chinese black mushrooms can be used interchangeably. Shiitake take well to grilling, roasting, stir-frying, and sautéing.

Index

First published in the USA by Time-Life Custom Publishing.

Originally published as Williams-Sonoma Lifestyles Series:
After Dinner (© 1998 Weldon Owen Inc.)
Chicken for Dinner (© 1998 Weldon Owen Inc.)
Classic Pasta at Home (© 1998 Weldon Owen Inc.)
Everyday Roasting (© 1998 Weldon Owen Inc.)
Fresh & Light (© 1998 Weldon Owen Inc.)
Holiday Celebrations (© 1998 Weldon Owen Inc.)
Soup for Supper (© 1998 Weldon Owen Inc.)
Vegetarian for All Seasons (© 1998 Weldon Owen Inc.)
Asian Flavors (© 1999 Weldon Owen Inc.)
Backyard Barbeque (© 1999 Weldon Owen Inc.)
Brunch Entertaining (© 1999 Weldon Owen Inc.)
Cooking From the Farmer's Market (© 1999 Weldon Owen Inc.)
Cooking for Yourself (© 1999 Weldon Owen Inc.)
Food & Wine Pairing (© 1999 Weldon Owen Inc.)
Holiday Cooking with Kids (© 1999 Weldon Owen Inc.)
Small Plates (© 1999 Weldon Owen Inc.)
Weekends with Friends (© 2000 Weldon Owen Inc.)

In collaboration with Williams-Sonoma Inc.
3250 Van Ness Avenue, San Francisco, CA 94109

Oxmoor
House.
OXMOOR HOUSE INC.
Oxmoor House books are distributed by Sunset Books
80 Willow Road, Menlo Park, CA 94025
Telephone: 650-321-3600 Fax 650-324-1532
Vice President/General Manager: Rich Smeby
National Accounts Manager/Special Sales: Brad Moses

Oxmoor House and Sunset Books are divisions of
Southern Progress Corporation

WILLIAMS-SONOMA
Founder and Vice-Chairman: Chuck Williams

WELDON OWEN INC.
Group Chief Executive Officer: John Owen
Chief Executive Officer and President: Terry Newell
Chief Operating Officer: Simon Fraser
Vice President Sales/Business Development: Amy Kaneko
Vice President International Sales: Stuart Laurence

Vice President and Creative Director: Gaye Allen
Vice President and Publisher: Hannah Rahill
Designer: Rachel Lopez Metzger
Managing Editor: Lisa Atwood
Senior Designer: Kara Church
Associate Editor: Juli Vendzules
Production Director: Chris Hemesath
Production Manager: Michelle Duggan
Color Manager: Teri Bell

Williams-Sonoma Appetizers was conceived and
produced by Weldon Owen Inc.
814 Montgomery Street, San Francisco, CA 94133
Copyright © 2007 Weldon Owen Inc.
and Williams-Sonoma Inc.

First printed in 2007.
10 9 8 7 6 5 4 3 2 1

ISBN-10: 0-8487-3194-8
ISBN-13: 978-0-8487-3194-6

Printed in China by Leefung-Asco Printers Ltd.

Authors: Georgeanne Brennan: Pages 16, 26, 30, 41, 55, 64, 94, 97, 101, 115, 124, 139, 157, 168, 179, 197, 215, 227, 233, 248, 286; Heidi Haughty Cusick: Pages 127, 140, 188, 198, 204; Lane Crowther: Pages 38, 119, 120, 132, 162, 180, 195, 223, 254, 257, 266; Janet Fletcher: Pages 80, 128, 135, 167; Joyce Goldstein: Pages 44, 100, 102, 116, 123, 153, 184, 187, 192, 196, 200, 207, 219, 224, 228, 231, 234, 236, 239, 240, 244, 247, 255, 261, 269, 273–274, 277–278, 282, 285; Pamela Sheldon Johns: Pages 34, 37, 67, 71, 76, 136, 212, 216, 237, 243, 251; Joyce Jue: 43, 47–48, 79, 88, 99, 105, 106, 191, 258, 270; Susan Manlin Katzman: Page 19; Betty Rosbottom: Pages 158, 171, 220, 262; Janeen Sarlin: 131, 165, 201, 211, 252; Phillip Stephen Schultz: Page 176; Marie Simmons: Pages 51, 203; Joanne Weir: Pages 15, 20, 22–23, 25, 29, 33, 40, 56, 59–60, 63, 68, 72, 83–84, 87, 90–91, 93, 96, 109–110, 147–148, 150, 154; Chuck Williams: Pages 75, 143–144, 161, 164, 172, 175, 208, 230, 265, 281.

Photographers: Richard Eskite, Joyce Oudkerk Pool, and Allan Rosenberg (recipe photography); Tucker+Hossler (cover).

Food Stylists: George Dolese, Andrea Lucich, Susan Massey, Pouké (recipe styling); Kevin Crafts (cover).

Weldon Owen would like to thank Ken DellaPenta, Melissa Eatough, and Sharon Silva for their expertise and hard work.